THE GROUP PROCESS AS A HELPING TECHNIQUE

Sheila Thompson and J. H. Kahn

With an Introduction by
Dame Eileen Younghusband D.B.E., J.P.

mmonwealth and International Library of Science Technology Engineering an d Liberal So

THE COMMONWEALTH AND INTERNATIONAL LIBRARY
Joint Chairmen of the Honorary Editorial Advisory Board

SIR ROBERT ROBINSON, O.M., F.R.S., LONDON
DEAN ATHELSTAN SPILHAUS, MINNESOTA

SOCIAL WORK DIVISION
General Editor: JEAN NURSTEN

THE GROUP PROCESS
AS A HELPING TECHNIQUE

361.4
T37

3.7 ✗

525

58408

THE GROUP PROCESS
AS A
HELPING TECHNIQUE

A TEXTBOOK FOR
SOCIAL WORKERS, PSYCHOLOGISTS, DOCTORS, TEACHERS
AND OTHER WORKERS IN COMMUNITY SERVICES

BY

SHEILA THOMPSON, A.A.P.S.W.

AND

J. H. KAHN, M.D., D.P.M.

WITH AN INTRODUCTION BY
DAME EILEEN YOUNGHUSBAND, D.B.E.

PERGAMON PRESS

OXFORD · NEW YORK · TORONTO

SYDNEY · BRAUNSCHWEIG

Pergamon Press Ltd., Headington Hill Hall, Oxford

Pergamon Press Inc., Maxwell House, Fairview Park, Elmsford, New York 10523

Pergamon of Canada Ltd., 207 Queen's Quay West, Toronto 1

Pergamon Press (Aust.) Pty. Ltd., 19a Boundary Street, Rushcutters Bay, N.S.W. 2011, Australia

Vieweg & Sohn GmbH, Burgplatz 1, Braunschweig

Copyright © 1970 Sheila Thompson & J. H. Kahn

All Rights Reserved. No part of this publication may be reproduced, stored in a retrieval system, or transmitted, in any form or by any means, electronic, mechanical, photocopying, recording or otherwise, without the prior permission of Pergamon Press Ltd.

First edition 1970

Library of Congress Catalog Card No. 79–124667

Printed in Great Britain by A. Wheaton & Co., Exeter

This book is sold subject to the condition
that it shall not, by way of trade, be lent,
resold, hired out, or otherwise disposed
of without the publisher's consent,
in any form of binding or cover
other than that in which
it is published.

08 016219 3 (flexicover)
08 016220 7 (hard cover)

In view of the fast growing complexity and scope of modern knowledge no one profession dealing with a range of human needs can make exclusive claims in relation to the others. Each has its essential function as well as its necessary overlap with others. This overlay is indeed required for intelligent co-operation and team-work. It should also enable a holistic approach to be made to the multiple needs of man.

Report of the Working Party on Social Workers in
the Local Authority Health and Welfare Services,
H.M.S.O. 1959.

This passage is reproduced here in the hope that the message will not be lost in the reorganisation and redistribution of the medical, social work, and educational services.

Our book is intended to deal with some of the areas of work which involve all of these services.

S. M. T.
J. H. K.

Contents

Editorial

THERE is a long tradition in Britain of social work with communities and groups, but professional social work training has been concerned with casework : understanding and helping the individual and his family. And even in casework, it is relatively recently that principles and methods common to all casework practice, irrespective of the setting, have been taught. Such social work education is called generic, as the principles and methods belong to the whole order of casework whether with the physically or mentally handicapped, or offenders, or deprived children and their families. This concept of generic training can be taken further, once the beginning worker has soundly grasped casework principles and method. Social workers are concerned with families as a group, and the family can act as a link between work with individuals and other clients in groups—whether young delinquents on probation, mothers' groups in a Family Service Unit, or psychiatric patients in hospital. Much emphasis has been given to group work, with the recognition that the clients' place is in the community, since the Mental Health Act, 1959. Renewed emphasis is given in the Report on Local Authority and Allied Personal Services (Seebohm Report, 1968), where it is stated that the trend towards group work would grow with the establishment of a social service department.

This book on the Group Process as a Helping Technique is the fifth in the series for social workers that has been developed during the past year. The book, however, will reach a wider public as it is put together with people in mind from other professional orientations who care, and want to help through using groups.

JEAN P. NURSTEN,
The University of Bradford.

Acknowledgement

WE WISH to express our gratitude to our teachers, to our colleagues, and to the members of the groups with which we have been associated in diverse capacities.

We should also like to acknowledge our debt to the group psychotherapists whose ideas have influenced our thinking, amongst whom special mention must be made of Dr. S. H. Foulkes.

S. M. T.
J. H. K.

Introduction

THE systematic and professional use of an understanding of group processes has been astonishingly slow to develop in teaching, in psychotherapy or in social work. Each has made its ritual bow to the powerful influences on the individual of group membership but tended to leave these influences professionally unexplored and unused. This is in marked contrast to advances in professional practice with individuals in psychiatry, clinical psychology and social work. It is to be hoped that this book, with its valuable analysis of the actual processes of Group Psychotherapy, Group Counselling, and Group Discussion, will help in redressing this imbalance.

The authors write from their own direct experience, although they are well aware of the contributions to the understanding of group processes which have come from other sources, since studies of group behaviour have multiplied in recent years, whether from within educational psychology, social psychology, psychiatry or sociology. This situation contrasts with casework, community work and some psychiatric practice where the sheer pressure of practice has resulted in a search for usable theory and itself led to action research.

To go back and try to disentangle the different trends is to discover that social group work has always been much more advanced, on a more friendly soil, in the United States than here. This is strange since the settlement movement was equally lively on both sides of the Atlantic in the early days of the century. But we in this country continued in our work with groups of young people and others to be fatally centred on achievement, on the tangible proofs of education, rather than on the growth of personality through satisfying group experiences. In the United States, on the other hand, John

Dewey's teaching about child-centred education spilled over into social work and, by the 1930's, social group work had become well recognised as a social work method comparable with, though differing from, casework. The result was that American social work teachers and practitioners began the systematic study of the actual processes at work in group interaction, the reciprocal influences of the individual and the group on each other, and of the way in which the understanding of these processes could be used to give particular groups of people a constructive experience of group membership. The aim was to increase their social abilities and confidence. Until after the Second World War, social group work was thought of in North America mainly as a means of enriching the social and recreational experiences of reasonably normal young people. None the less, there were experiments in the use of group work skills in psychiatric settings.

After the Second World War, new strands emerged and the whole scene has become, at the same time, more diffuse and more coherent in the years since 1945. One source of subsequent developments here came from the group of psychiatrists who pioneered group therapy in civilian resettlement units for returning prisoners of war. On the other side of the Atlantic, Bruno Bettleheim, Fritz Redl, Eva Burmeister and others were experimenting with "creative group living" for severely disturbed or deprived young people. In another direction, it was discovered that small group discussion could bring about changes in attitudes which were tenaciously resistant to any amount of well-presented information or persuasion. The work of Moreno (sociograms), of Slavson (leadership styles) and of Elton Mayo and his colleagues (the Hawthorne Experiment) had some influence on youth work, resulting in more self-government, and an added belief in the value of the small group and "leading from behind". Indeed, the impetus to evolve the practice of social group work has probably come largely from belief in democratic values.

In the meantime, in addition to work with disturbed and

delinquent young people and adults in residential situations, "unattached" workers have begun to follow up the pioneer work of Whyte, *Street Corner Society* (1943) and others by making relations with and studying the interactions of small groups of deviant youths. Later, work with unattached youth spread to this country and resulted in such studies as *The Unattached* (Mary Morse, 1965), *Working with Unattached Youth* (Joan Tash and George Getschins, 1967), and *Stress and Release on an Urban Estate* (John Spencer, 1964). These were all based on detailed recordings of what actually happened over a span of time in the relations within the group, with the participant observer, and with the often hostile larger community. They were not related to any particular psychological or sociological theory of group relations.

In the meantime there were various studies of the "inmate system" in prisons, mental hospitals and children's treatment institutions in the U.S.A. For example, *Cottage Six* (Howard Polsky, 1962) showed the futility of individual casework treatment unrelated to the processes at work in the group. In this country, *Growth to Freedom* (Derek Miller, 1964), an action study of homeless Borstal boys in a hostel, illustrated the use of psychoanalytic concepts in group treatment. Group Counselling was also beginning to be used in prisons and other institutions, primarily as a means of bringing about attitude changes.

Important new knowledge also resulted from sociological studies of group and intergroup relations, especially in industry. This helped to clarify the formal and informal structure and communication system in large organisations. Other studies of culturally determined attitudes, values, and assumptions further illuminated group behaviour and showed the importance of this dimension as well as an understanding of individual and group psychology. Role theory also helped to clarify the roles in which different members of a group might be cast, or cast themselves, and the effect of this on group behaviour. Other studies began to show how groups of people behave under conditions of extreme stress.

The development of "T" groups originated in the work of A. K. Rice and others at the Tavistock Institute of Human Relations, *Learning for Leadership* (1965), in operational research on relations in industrial settings. The technique, which can be dangerous in the hands of untrained people, is based upon helping members of small work groups to become aware of what is going on in the "here and now" in their relations with each other, on the assumption that the often painful awareness of this will make them more sensitive in other group situations. This "sensitivity training", as it is also known, is now widely used in some forms of professional education—for example, in social work courses.

The concept of the therapeutic community, which originated in the work of Maxwell Jones, *Social Psychiatry* (1962), is spreading to institutions other than mental hospitals and has resulted in new perceptions about the powerful effects of group and inter-group relations between "inmates" and staff in promoting or retarding individual progress. In short, we are beginning to see that conscious use of the group milieu may be as important in treatment as individual procedures or as in good physical care.

Yet another strand comes from community development projects, especially where sociological or psychological concepts are being used to motivate local people to learn how to work together to bring about some change in their situation.

All the foregoing groups are either task oriented—that is to say, they have specific objectives in view—or process oriented, existing primarily for individual or group fulfilment. At the present day, carefully selected or spontaneous groups are found in many social agencies. Examples are foster parent or would-be adoptive parent groups in children's departments, partly information giving and partly to explore the meaning of a particular experience. Others are self-help groups—for example, parents of handicapped children who may gain strength from association with each other.

This brief, and by no means comprehensive, survey shows

our new-found knowledge about, and awareness of, group relations as a therapeutic tool, not only for those who are in need of treatment but also as a means of enriching the life experience of ordinary people. Since this is essentially a psycho-social process, it is surprising that training for social group work should still be at an embryo stage in this country. The method is being used in the social field either by untrained workers or otherwise trained workers, or else by caseworkers whose knowledge and professional skill need extending if they are to be used effectively in often highly charged group relations. It must be emphasised, as the authors rightly stress, that damage as well as good can arise from group interaction.

What Dr. Kahn and Mrs. Thompson say about the need for psychiatrists to be trained in group processes applies with equal force to social workers. Teachers, doctors, health visitors and others working for educational or therapeutic purposes through group discussion and participation also need to have at least basic knowledge and skill if they are to be effective.

This book should give them a better grasp of both the knowledge and the skill because the authors are able to present so cogently from their own experiences some of the processes involved in the actual working with groups.

DAME EILEEN YOUNGHUSBAND, D.B.E.

CHAPTER 1

Why Groups?

"LET'S have a Group!" This is a suggestion which is now frequently heard when social workers meet together to discuss developments in the work of their agencies and departments. These are agencies and departments which traditionally offer help by means of individual interviews conducted in private. The suggestion is that, in some instances, individual interviews might be replaced by a group meeting in which a number of clients would come together with a social worker to discuss their problems.

Despite the fact that most social work departments are understaffed, the suggestion is not made primarily in order to achieve an economy in scarce professional resources. Rather, the suggestion is made in the belief that group work can bring a new and powerful resource into the helping process, a resource that is not present in the one-to-one interview situation. This resource is the group situation itself, and the "forces" which operate in it. These are forces which are present in every group, whatever its purpose and composition, though for the most part they go unrecognised; indeed, it is only of recent years, and for particular purposes, that they have begun to be identified and studied. The suggestion "Let's have a Group!" is made in the belief that these forces can be understood and utilised by a group leader whose aim is the provision of help for the personal problems of individuals and families.

It is not only social workers who are interested in the possibilities which group work opens up. There are many

1

members of other professions whose work it is to meet with people in groups, be it in school, hospital, prison, church, or youth club. There are other workers who provide a service for individuals, and who are beginning to consider that this service might be augmented and improved through the use of groups. Like social workers, these are people who employ well-established techniques within their own different professional frameworks. The existence of the professional framework is a necessary prerequisite. Group work, as we are envisaging it, cannot exist *in vacuo*, but can be used to provide an extension of existing practice in work with people who come, singly or together, seeking help.

It must be assumed that each potential group worker will have an original professional framework and will be capable of a disciplined approach to any group work that he undertakes. His knowledge of group work will enable him to co-operate with members of other professions who are also working in this field. It would, however, be an impoverishment if entering into group work separated him from his original colleagues. A teacher, for example, who receives a group work training will have added a new dimension to his work with his pupils and their families, but he will remain a teacher. Similarly, a clergyman might be able to provide himself with an additional framework for some of the pastoral duties which are traditionally his, but he would not acquire a new profession.

To many social workers, in particular, recent developments within their professional thinking are beginning to make group work seem an inevitable and logical extension. There has been a shift in emphasis from individual to family psychology which is habituating social workers to think of individuals, not in isolation, but as members of interacting groups of people whose every action affects and is affected by others. A child has his parents, a pupil his teachers, and in the past it has been more usual to think of the individual relationship of the child with either parent, or with a particular teacher, than to trace the way in which the development of the child depends upon the family dynamics or upon the total interaction of children and teachers in the class or in the school. It is now recognised that for many purposes the unit of relationship is the group and involves many people. In general, personal problems arise in groups, manifest themselves in group situations, and each problem is intermeshed with the problems of others. This shift in emphasis prepares the way for a treatment situation in which the single relationship of an individual interview is replaced by the multi-dimensional relationships of a group.

However, social workers, and all others aspiring to work with people in and through groups, must also look outside their own profession. They must be able to make use of concepts not originally their own, and integrate these concepts with their existing skills. The relevant concepts are those of dynamic group psychology, which are derived from the practice of group psychotherapists of different schools, and which alone enable us to understand the nature of groups and the forces operating in them. It is through these concepts that it becomes possible to use the group situation in a conscious and disciplined way. They are complex in the extreme, and they cannot be transferred wholesale from the psycho-therapeutic setting in which they were first developed. Their use in other settings, by other workers, raises problems which can only be solved through a consideration of the ultimate aims for which the work is being carried out. Thus any profession seeking to extend into the field of group work needs to be doubly sure of its own professional foundations, on which its own system of group work will have to be built.

The interest in group work methods is not without its dangers. The group situation contains forces which can be harmful as well as helpful to the individual, and unfocused group work can be doubly hazardous. The extension of group work only has value if the impetus comes from within each separate profession, and arises from the actual needs of that profession as they are seen in its day-to-day practice. Each profession must supply its own focus and its own boundaries.

We are suggesting that ideas derived originally from group psychotherapy, which have been developed by, amongst others, social workers, can be, and will be, extended into yet other fields occupied by other professions. In order to clear the stage, and before proceeding to discuss the concepts of group work themselves, we wish to elaborate in a little detail some of the issues which are raised by the process of communication across professional boundaries, by the extension of work into areas that are occupied by more than one profession, and by the participation of members of different professions in one training course.

The communication of ideas from one profession to another is an important theme throughout this book, which is itself a product of interdisciplinary communication. One of the authors is a psychiatric social worker, the other a psychiatrist. Neither could have written it alone. The book makes use of concepts basic to both professions, and defines fields of work in which these concepts have a practical application. It is addressed to members of the authors' professions and to many others. In order to write this book, the authors have had to make themselves aware of the issues that arise when a member of one profession is communicating ideas to members of another.

It has become a commonplace to speak of "the multi-disciplinary approach" in social and medical services. However, there are many problems in the actual sharing of work and ideas when members of different professions join together in a common task. The same problems exist wherever professional workers receive a training in which other professions are brought into the teaching programme. In the various courses for social workers there may be lectures from psychiatrists, psychologists, doctors, administrators, and from many others who are not practising social workers and who therefore are teaching something other than social work. It is left to the students to make some integration of entirely separate systems of thought. Doctors and teachers are in the same plight in their student days, and even after qualification they continue to be confronted with competing (and conflicting) ways of meeting old and new problems. Only in some exceptional cases are there university courses in which medical, psychological, and social work students share a basic training in the behavioural sciences.

When members of different professions meet in a situation in which one is designated teacher and the other student, what does one ask of the other? Is the student expected to take within himself the attitudes and ethos of the one who is cast in the role of teacher? Is he expected to join the teacher's profession? Is he expected to become the teacher's disciple, subordinate, or rival? Is the purpose of the encounter to develop something new that will become the property of his own profession; or can they, both together, develop something new in a fresh area which they both can share? For where members of two different professions meet, each could and should have something to learn from the other; and the roles of teacher and student can frequently be reversed.

Psychiatrists, psychologists, and social workers are very often cast in the role of teachers of other professions. Willingly or unwillingly, many of them accept the role. There are few professions today that do not face demands from their own public for an extension of their work into areas which are concerned with feelings, motivations, and relationships. Psychiatrists, psychologists, and social workers belong to separate professions with different theoretical and practical training, but they are believed to have, in common, some special knowledge in these areas. They are frequently called upon to deal personally with disturbances of feelings and behaviour in individuals who are referred to them by others. Sometimes they are expected to be able to teach those others the special skills with which they are credited.

A psychiatrist, for example, may take part in the teaching of social workers or social work students, but he does not teach them to be psychiatrists; neither does he teach them how to be social workers, for that would not be within his competence. In some of the more progressive medical schools social workers teach undergraduate and post-graduate medical students : this, in turn, is not intended to teach them how to become social workers, nor how to become doctors. Each presents a method of approach to topics that are of common concern, with an awareness that there is a point of contact at which something new is going to be created.

The authors believe that there are three requisites for someone who is teaching members of another profession :

1. Respect for oneself.
2. Respect for the immediate occasion.
3. Respect for the profession of those with a student role.

The teacher's respect for himself has to include his attitude to his own profession. The psychiatrist who teaches other professions should not denigrate psychiatry. It is his original training as a psychiatrist that gives him his authority to teach. It is his capacity to see the relevance of this to other fields that justifies an invitation to teach other professions. However, he must not become so far infatuated with the new applications that he ceases to acknowledge and value the work that is carried out in the mainstream of his profession.

The respect for the occasion includes punctuality; an appropriate amount of preparation for each meeting, which may involve the collection of factual material about some topic or official document, and which also includes the totality of his professional experience; and the devotion of his attention to the communications from the members of his class or group.

The respect for the other profession must be genuine, and it requires that the lecturer should not imply that his students will provide an inferior substitute for what he himself would do. There is a tendency to suggest that, because psychiatrists and some kinds of social worker are in short supply, some of their work should be done by others with "lesser skills". The message frequently is "I haven't time, so will you take on some of my cases?" It can never be satisfactory for members of a profession to be considered to be working as second-best on jobs that ought, in an ideal society, to be done by someone else. The purpose of the teaching should be to make the job into *the actual property* of the people who are going to undertake it.

The position is no better when someone of an academic discipline undermines the valuation of work which has a practical aim. There are those who use the word "scientific" only for the organisation of data which can be measured. Such people try to distinguish between observations which are objective, and which therefore are absolute, and those which, being subjective, depend upon value systems. This in itself is a value system, in which the student's ultimate profession, if directed to personal social service, is given a lower valuation than engagement in the making of "scientific surveys".

A practical example of the problems which occur at the meeting of disciplines occurred when a psychiatrist was given the assignment of conducting a series of discussion groups with medical, nursing, and social work colleagues working for the same local authority. At the first meeting with a group of assistant medical officers of health, not knowing how to begin, he asked the assembled medical officers, "What do you expect of me?" Immediately one of them replied, "That you should understand our work." The psychiatrist replied, "That's fair enough", and then it occurred to him to add, "But it is more important that I should know mine." As the discussion developed it became apparent that the medical officers expected him to claim that he knew more about their work than they did themselves, and they had come prepared to challenge such a claim. They knew that they had problems with their work and that they wanted help. But they were doubtful whether it was possible to get this help from someone who, whatever his claims, could not have had their experience with the problems that they were going to discuss. What then, they wondered, did he have to offer? The contribution that was offered was the psychiatrist's own tentative thoughts about problems which were new to him. It was the fact that the problems were new to him that made it possible for him to respond. He had his own experience, the medical officers had theirs, but they were going to deal with topics on which they could share their ignorance. Some of the thoughts that would arise would be new to all of them. What the psychiatrist had to offer was not his greater experience of some particular problem. His contribution was his method of approach. He did not expect the members of the group to exchange their own methods for his, but to look at their methods anew in a wider context.

The very nature of the problems which were brought to these meetings made it appropriate for discussion of them to take place in such a group. Many of the problems concerned patients who already were in contact with various specialist medical services and with a number of different social work departments. The problems were those which straddled the different professions and which were provided for, often very inadequately, by a number of statutory and voluntary services. Many of the issues referred to cases for which the practical decisions had already been made at meetings of co-ordinating committees. In this new group, the participants offered different viewpoints on any problem which was brought into discussion and they were also able to recall similar or comparable problems. The re-formulations that were made were not the exclusive property of the one who suggested them at the discussion, nor of the leader, but they were, in varying degrees, the property of the whole group.

There are different problems when such groups contain a bigger variety of professions. Some homogeneity exists even if only in the devotion of attention to the topics that arise. In some cases the primary purpose of the group meeting is for the members themselves to gain experience in the conducting of groups. Even so, when different professions share a group experience of in-service training, they all retain their own professional identity and do not become members of an amorphous collection of group workers with no roots else-where. Group work is not a practice which stands by itself, separate from the other work that each one does.

In this book we deal with many of the general principles of group work as we understand them. The book provides an example of the way in which ideas from a variety of sources have to be brought together. The reader will make his own selections from these ideas, will follow his own associations of thought, and will take himself into directions that he himself will choose.

Each group worker will need to preserve and develop his original professional framework and will need a disciplined approach to any group work that he undertakes. His know-ledge of group work will enable him to co-operate with members of other professions who are also entering into this field. The three levels of respect referred to above have an application to every group worker. They can be re-specified as respect for his own professional identity, respect for the practical procedures that he undertakes, and respect for his colleagues in other professions and for those whom he serves.

CHAPTER 2

Setting the Scene

PROXIMITY is not enough to turn a number of different objects into a group. There are other requirements that have to be fulfilled. If they are to be considered a group, the different objects must contain some property in common, and they must also be related to each other in such a way that it is possible to consider them as a single entity. There must also be an observer, since such forming of objects into a group is a function of their perception. It is the observer who recognises the common property and who finds the unifying relationship, and who thus creates a group.

There are several trees on the skyline, more than a pair, yet not enough for us to describe them as a wood. We recognise that they are all trees, and that they have this property in common with each other and in distinction from the other objects around them. They are so placed in relation to each other that we are able to pick them out from their surroundings and consider them as a whole. Our perception of the trees turns them into a group.

This concept of a group is similar to the concepts used by the Gestalt psychologists who base their ideas of perception on the capacity which human beings have to organise the elements of perceived objects into a composite whole.

As with trees, so it is with people. A group is bigger than a couple and smaller than a crowd. In our perception of groups of people, we look for a point in common and a

10

relationship that unites the different individuals together as parts of a single whole.

What the common point might be, and what type of relationship we would look for, would depend upon our context. A painter, interested in visual properties, may "see men as trees, walking", finding a common element in the shape that each one makes, and a spatial relationship between them that creates a unity. Another context, that of dynamic psychology, has other requirements, and seeks different resemblances and relationships. The common factor may be found in a shared purpose or concern, of which all the individual members are aware; and the relationship, linking all the parts of the group together in a unique way, may be found in the psychological interaction which follows upon the shared purpose. People may be turned into a group through the activity of an external observer, but equally they may become a group through their own recognition of each other.

A number of people sitting in a railway compartment might be considered a group by a painter able to fit them all into one composition. But if each sits reading a newspaper, or sleeping, if there is little or no communication between them, they cannot be considered a group in any psychological sense. Suppose, however, that there is a breakdown, the train is delayed, and their immediate future becomes uncertain. Under the impact of this external event, they exchange and share feelings of indignation, anxiety, and distress (and despite the discomfort, these feelings may have overtones which are not unpleasant). Each communicates something, and each responds to the communications of the others. These communications and responses can be looked upon as a pattern of interaction, relating each part to each other part. This pattern of interaction is the psychological counterpart to the relationship of shapes and colours with which the painter is concerned. For us, it is the existence and recognition of this interaction that turns a collection of people into a group.

We use the Gestalt psychologists' explanation of the way

people discover patterns in unrelated objects to illustrate the fact that we need some dynamic systems of psychology to explain the pattern of group behaviour that we perceive when people meet and interact together.

Thus a number of people congregate, sharing some purpose, interest, or concern, and stay together long enough for the development of a network of relationships which includes them all. Recognition of this network brings the concept of a group. Each member of the group, though he may continue to behave in ways which are characteristic of him, is influenced by the behaviour of each of the others and also by the prevailing mood or climate which is present in the group at any moment of time. This mood, or climate, is something to which he contributes but which he cannot control.

The group may consist of a number of colleagues having a drink together after work, a reunion of old students, a discussion group, a committee meeting, a psychotherapeutic group, or any one of the small face-to-face gatherings in which most of us spend a large part of our working lives. After such a meeting, one may look back and wonder why each person behaved as he did, why one member talked so much and another so little, why one was listened to so eagerly and another relatively ignored. Why was this topic pursued with interest and that topic allowed to drop? Why was so and so never mentioned, and such and such only treated flippantly? Why was everyone so lively at one point, and so much quieter a little later on? What forces, in fact, determine the proceedings of a group, and, supposing there are such forces, how can one begin to study and understand them?

A student of individual psychology might focus upon the behaviour of each individual member in turn, and attempt to give separate explanations for each one in turn in the light of what he can learn about him. But he would find this approach insufficient to account for the complete pattern of events, or to answer the questions posed above. It might be compared with an attempt to explain the shifting pattern of a kaleidoscope by taking the tube to pieces and listing the fragments found inside. Something more than this is needed. It becomes apparent that in studying groups we are not dealing with a collection of different pieces of behaviour happening in juxtaposition, but with a complex and dynamic interaction.

In order to try to understand this interaction, it is necessary to take all the individual pieces of behaviour, the contributions of each different member, and treat them as if they were parts of a meaningful whole. In order to do this, we have to make certain assumptions about the nature of groups. We have to form a concept of the Group (and just this once we spell the word with a capital "G")[1] as a separate entity, to ascribe forces to it, and even to endow it with capacities for decision and action. We have to do this in order to describe and explain certain aspects of human behaviour, and we are entitled to do so as long as we do not forget that the group is an abstraction. Such a concept can be compared with the many other concepts in psychology which do not refer to anything with an actual, concrete existence, but which provide the language which is necessary for the description of psychological phenomena. The Superego, for example, is not a material object; it is an abstract concept which embodies inferences from observations of behaviour and perceptions of experience.

If we treat this concept of the group too concretely, it may lead us into another error, namely the naïve transfer of properties which belong to the individual and to the group as a whole. Some of the mechanisms familiar in individual psychology may have their counterparts at a group level (and we shall presently be considering ambivalence in this connection), but their presence cannot be assumed, and each needs to be discovered afresh.

For our purposes, it is necessary to consider the group as

[1] A small "g" will be used to refer to a group on its own, but capitals will be used for the labels which the authors give to distinctive group systems.

a separate psychological entity, but this does not alter the fact that it has no existence apart from the activity of its individual members. Any property or activity that we may ascribe to the group arises solely through the normal psychodynamics and the psychopathologies of people meeting together, through the ways in which they interrelate, and through their reactions to the external realities of the situation in which they find themselves. The activity of the whole and the activity of the parts must both be studied.

If we are to assume that some connection exists between all the events taking place in a group, then we must also assume that, at some level, forces exist and exert an influence over every single thing that happens. To these forces we give the name of group processes. These processes must belong to the group situation itself; they are created by the group, and they occur inevitably whenever several people meet and form a relationship with each other. So if one is to understand the meaning of the behaviour of any particular person in a group context at a moment in time, an exhaustive knowledge of that person is not enough; one must also look for the processes operating in the group which will have played a part in eliciting that behaviour. These processes are not usually within the conscious awareness of the group members who are participating in them, but they may be more readily apparent to a detached observer.

To illustrate this point, let us consider a summary of events at one particular group meeting. A number of students meet together for a drink on the evening before an important exam. Several of them immediately start to talk about their work in a flippant and frivolous manner. Two of them begin to discuss an academic point, but the discussion soon peters out and they fall silent. A reference to exhaustion due to hours spent in study is ignored. A shipwreck, reported in the day's news, is mentioned, with the fact that some of the ship's crew were drowned because they could not all fit into the lifeboat. An absent student with a reputation for hard work and academic success is mentioned, and criticised as unhelpful and unfriendly. Several students discuss his way of life with pity and with some contempt, deploring its narrowness and lack of social and sexual content. There is an argument about payment for the drinks, a refusal to let any one person undertake this, and finally an agreement that each member should contribute an identical amount. No one seems to want to leave, and they stay until closing-time.

If we look for some underlying process linking together every single separate incident that took place at this meeting, we find an attempt to reconcile two distinct and incompatible sets of feelings. On the one hand, there is the wish that the group should continue to exist and provide the companionship and support of peers; on the other hand, there are competitive and disruptive feelings, the fears of arousing envy and hostility in others by examination successes, or alternatively, of experiencing envy and hostility oneself on the occasion of failure. These are the feelings that are activated or emphasised by the actual group situation, and whatever other needs and preoccupations the individual members have, they all share these feelings to some extent. Thus we find an area of common ground where the different problems of individuals meet in a group problem. The behaviour of each individual at this particular group meeting can be regarded as part of an overall pattern of behaviour which has as its aim the reconciliation of the two opposing sets of feelings and which represents the group's struggle to survive under the pressure of disruptive forces.

In the light of our assumptions, the events taking place at the students' meeting can be interpreted in the following way. The group at first decides that exams are not to be taken seriously, and therefore the threat to the group can be treated as if it does not exist. This solution is not at first unanimous, and some pressure has to be exerted to make it so. The students' wish to remain all in the same boat, and their fears that the group may break up violently, are then expressed symbolically, since the anxieties are too strong to be dealt with effectively by denial and must be expressed outwardly in some other way. They then find that they can broach their competitive feelings more directly, without endangering the group, by denigrating an absent rival, and at the same time maintain the fiction that none of them is actually seeking academic success. No one is allowed to take on the superior position of host. At the end of the meeting anxieties and fears are still present, since nothing has happened to relieve them, and a sense that a threat still exists makes it difficult for the group to disband.

This interpretation is based on the assumptions that we are using in order to have a method by which to examine group behaviour. To sum up, we assume that all the different events taking place in a group, though contributed by different people, can be treated as if they were the product of a single entity. We assume that these events are all connected through the operation of forces known as "group processes" which are a property of the group as a whole. We assume that, through the operation of group processes, attempts are made to reconcile the opposing tendencies which are present in every group, and which by their opposition arouse anxiety in the members and even threaten the group's continued existence.

Anyone familiar with the literature on group work will recognise that these assumptions belong to a particular dynamic viewpoint which derives ultimately from psychoanalysis. We will return to these assumptions and to their origins in the chapter on Group Psychotherapy; for the moment we are simply stating them in order to set the scene for what follows.

In our example, the group of students had from the beginning one over-riding preoccupation in which all members shared, and it also had very little of the structure that can impose formal patterns, and through its formality hinder the spontaneous development and expression of a common group them. In other, more structured, groups we are likely to find that the group processes appear more complex and devious, and are influenced by a greater number of variables.

In order to consider the processes taking place in any particular group situation, one has to consider first of all the expressed purpose for which the group is meeting. Every gathering that is more than an unrelated collection of individuals will have a purpose, as the purpose of our students was the enjoyment of the companionship of their fellows. This purpose supplies a reason for meeting, establishing a framework and a context, and providing members with roles to play and expectations about the behaviour of other members; it may also impose a considerable degree of control over the proceedings.

A committee, convened to carry out a specific task, will need to have a structure designed to further this task and to exclude irrelevant elements. There will be a leader, or chairman, an agenda, and rules of procedure. Members will know that a certain type of behaviour is expected of them, and equally they will have expectations about the behaviour of the other members. If one looks at the record of the proceedings of a committee meeting, one would expect, and one might find, a greater coherence in the discussion, and a greater consistency in individual behaviour, than is usual in less structured groups. In this situation, as in all group situations, the group processes play their part, but their operation is likely to be more difficult to detect.

A social gathering, on the other hand, will have another framework. There will be no chairman, although there may be a host. There will be no agenda or rules of procedure, but there will be certain conventions influencing the way in which people behave and their expectations of the behaviour of others. The purpose of the meeting is enjoyable social intercourse, and the members will be expected to behave pleasantly and refrain from introducing any disturbing elements which might interfere with the enjoyment, or disrupt the harmony, of the group.

It seems that it is necessary for our comfort that the groups in which we take part should have a structure, which can

impose some control over what may take place, and set som
limits to the behaviour of ourselves and of others. It coul
be frightening to be in a situation where there seems to b
no form of control, where we can have no firm expectation
about what may happen, or where we do not know how w
ourselves are expected to behave. Such fears have been show
to exist in experimental leaderless groups, and in groups tha
are kept unstructured for a psychotherapeutic purpose.
Typically, in the beginning stage of these groups, there i
a period in which the members experience considerabl
anxiety; and they may try to press someone into the role o
leader, or attempt to devise some rules of procedure or agree
conventions of behaviour, even where this is quite inappropriate

Within the group structure, which may be firm or weak
explicit or implicit, are the individual members, each wit
his own psychological make-up, his own problems, and hi
own needs.

Every one of us is driven by certain emotional needs
Though we may not be conscious of the way in which the
influence our conduct, we all try to arrange our lives an
our relationships with other people so that these needs ca
be satisfied. We are each of us aware that we feel more a
home in certain situations and less at home in others. We lik
to play certain roles, to make certain types of relationships
and to be treated in certain ways. We are attracted to th
company of people who will allow us, or encourage us, t
behave in the way we wish, and who will give us the response
we seek. Wherever we are, we try to influence or manipulat
our associates so as to elicit from them the behaviour that th
satisfaction of our needs requires. We try to avoid situation
that we find unsatisfactory, or disturbing, or frustrating. I
we cannot avoid such situations, we look for some way t
change them or to lessen their impact. These basic emotiona
needs, which determine so much of our behaviour, in group

[1] Ezriel, H., A psychoanalytic approach to group treatmen
B.J.M.P., Vol. XXIII, Parts 1 and 2, 1950.

as in other situations, have their origins in our constitutional endowment and in our earliest relationships, and are shaped and influenced, modified or confirmed, by all our subsequent experiences.

Different needs will be activated by different circumstances. When a person is with a group of other people, the situation in itself and his feelings about the other people present, will determine which of his habitual needs he will experience and how he will endeavour to satisfy them. His behaviour will also be influenced by his feelings about the group itself, and the relationship prevailing between the group and the outside world.

To take a single instance : in a group meeting one member is lively and vivacious, responding to every topic and entertaining the gathering with his wit and fund of stories. This could be part of a characteristic pattern of behaviour which he habitually employs in such situations; if an interpretation for it is sought, it might be found in terms of early experiences which have made him equate lack of notice with lack of love and feel frustrated if he is not given attention. Alternatively, this behaviour might be the result of inter-relationships in this particular group and be specific to this situation; there may be a woman present whom he particularly wishes to impress, or a man who arouses strong competitive feelings. At another level, it could represent his reaction to a particular topic under discussion; he might want to divert attention from this topic, or to ensure that it is only treated flippantly. Finally his behaviour may be the result of his feelings about the group as a whole; a wish to keep it in existence because it is serving some need, juxtaposed with a fear that it is going to break up. At social gatherings similar behaviour is sometimes shown by anxious hosts.

How our man actually behaves will depend upon the other people present, each of whom will also be trying to arrange matters so that a predominant need is met. His behaviour will help, or hinder, the attempts of the others, and so will meet with support or discouragement in varying degrees. If one considers marriage as a permanent group of two, one can observe unions that appear to bring together pairs of complementary needs : to talk and to be talked to, to dominate and to submit, to protect and to be protected. These marriages may be harmonious, but are hardly likely to encourage personal growth and development since they provide no stimulus for change; in fact, the success of such a marriage may depend upon the maintenance of existing behaviour patterns. It does not seem probable that Jack Spratt and his wife ever changed their eating habits.

Such a consistent dovetailing of needs is not to be expected in a group situation. There we find constant adaptation and change as each member tries to influence the others to behave in a way favourable to his own particular and personal requirements. The more structured the group, and the more stereotyped the roles that the members are expected to play the less apparent will be the tensions and needs that each individual brings into the group. The needs will be there, and they will exert some influence, but they will be masked by the formal procedure and there will be less opportunity for them to obtrude into personal relationships.

No one will remain for long in a situation in which his needs are not met in some way or in some degree. If he is unable to influence the group to provide him even with some minimal satisfactions, then he will leave. The committee member whose needs are only satisfied when he is in a predominant position will aspire to be elected chairman. If unsuccessful in this, he may through hard work be able to establish a position for himself as an authority on some aspect of the subject at issue or he may become leader or spokesman of a minority group. If unable to obtain any of these satisfactions he may find fault with the committee's composition, terms of reference, or method of procedure, declaring it unworkable (which by now it very well may have become). If attendance is compulsory and he is unable to leave, he will perhaps withdraw into sleep or daydreams, or he may express his dissatisfactions through overt or covert destructive behaviour aimed at damaging or ending the group. Such destructive behaviour would be satisfying his newest and most pressing need, a need that has been activated by the specific reactions he has encountered in the group. It is not necessarily a position of comfort that is being sought; there may even be some who find a perverse satisfaction in demonstrating that none can satisfy them.

This example, illustrating the disruptive effect of a single unsatisfied group member, is likely to be familiar to those experienced in committees, and, equally, those experienced in committees will realise that this is only part of the story. It leaves out of account the constructive and cohesive forces within the group forming the committee, expressed in the consensus of opinion and the decisions which lead to action. It is this aspect which gets recorded in the minutes. The destructive forces operating in the group are not likely to be observed as such, and certainly not in the terms that we have used. The individual expression of such forces is more likely to be described, and may even find approval, under such labels as "sticking to one's principles" or "upholding the rights of minorities". A group that accepts such labels is, in fact, offering its destructive forces a legitimate means of expression, and it may be able to contain them in this way.

Despite its complex motivations, our behaviour usually remains appropriate to the different situations in which we find ourselves. We observe regulations and conventions, we pay some respect to the personal needs of others, and we still manage to achieve some satisfactions of our own. If a particular need is so compelling that it must be expressed, and if it cannot find expression through approved behaviour, then we have to behave in unapproved ways, and we run the risk of being designated unconventional, unreliable, eccentric, maladjusted, ill, or simply mad or bad. But most people are able to function at more than one level, satisfying at the same time, and through the same actions, their own needs and the expectations both of society in general and of their own immediate company.

If it is to continue in existence, and if it is to retain all its members, a group has to make some provision for the needs of each of the individuals who compose it, conflicting though these needs may be. Therefore the total proceedings of any group meeting can be seen, at one level, as a compromise which contains some part of the personal preoccupations of each member and which goes some way to meet the requirements of each. This is a dynamic position, and we mean by this that the compromise is continually being adjusted as the interaction taking place among the group members stimulates the perception of new needs and offers new solutions.

The success of the man who seeks to dominate the group will depend upon the way in which the other members react. His attempt might be welcomed by some for complex and personal reasons, and may be justified in terms of providing the group with a new direction, giving a firmer lead, introducing new ideas, or changing an existing unsatisfactory position. For converse reasons, it could be resisted by others. If there is open competition for leadership, then the group will only survive if it is able to find a way of accommodating these rivalries. Such competition would pose a problem for individual members; it also poses a problem for the group as a whole, and one must look at the total pattern of behaviour in the group to see the way in which this problem is met. One of the possible solutions would be for all members to take turns. This could be formalised in arrangements for different members to take the chair in rotation; informally, it could just happen that each member finds himself taking the lead successively while the other members acquiesce. Certain provocative topics which stimulate rivalry might be quietly dropped, as if by some silent agreement. Alternatively, some member, who is not himself involved in the leadership conflict, might find himself being placed in the position of arbiter and referee. These different patterns of group behaviour can be explained as alternative possible solutions to a problem belonging to the group as a whole; they only provide solutions to individual problems at the point where each individual problem and the group problem meet. They are not necessarily reached through any conscious decision. Rather, they are reached through the operation of the group processes which shape the proceedings of the group into a form that will serve as common ground, where the needs of each can meet and achieve some satisfaction.

It is this need to reconcile opposing drives, present in every group situation, which, according to our view, brings the group processes into existence. These group processes are complicated in the extreme. No observer can stand so far outside them as to be able to understand them all. It is necessary to force upon them the simplification of basic laws. These laws are found in the assumption we make that there are regularities in the group processes, no matter in what form they show themselves. Such an assumption is made by all writers on group work, and, in fact, there are comparable assumptions which underly every attempt to study the world in which we live. Science is based upon two acts of faith : firstly, there is the belief that the universe can be understood, and secondly, there is the belief that the same causes have the same effects. These beliefs are not subject to proof or disproof. An alternative set of beliefs would be, firstly, that the universe can never be completely understood, and secondly, that every event is unique. But in order to study science, we have to be content with the assumptions that serve us for the time being and hand over our doubts to the philosophers who open up new dimensions of enquiry.

To return to our particular concern with the limited subject of group processes, we believe that it is possible to provide a working basis by assuming that two fundamental and conflicting drives exist in every group, originating in two fundamental drives present in every individual : on the one hand there is the wish to be separate, and on the other hand there is the wish to be one of a group. Both these components are always present, though not necessarily in equal amounts.

The quality and strength of these drives in any individual will owe something to his constitutional make-up and to his previous history as well as to the nature of the group situation in which he finds himself. We all of us try to obtain, at one and the same time, the advantages of belonging and of not belonging. We conform to the customs and standards of our immediate social group, but within this conformity we try to establish the fact that we are different. We fear loneliness and isolation in being separate, and we fear loss of personal identity and of freedom in being one of a crowd. Anyone who seeks to be the leader of a group is seeking a situation in which he can emphasise an extreme degree of separateness while still maintaining membership of the group.

The existence of these two opposite drives is shown in the two conflicting attitudes towards groups that one meets in our culture. On the one hand, one finds the belief that the group is inimical to the individual, and that membership of a group entails a surrender of part of one's personal identity, a suppression of individuality, a loss of uniqueness, which is to be deplored. On the other hand, one finds an advocacy of group membership as containing a cure for all manner of social and psychological ills, from delinquency to widowhood. Clubs and associations proliferate to meet all tastes and needs, and are regarded as being beneficial to both individuals and to society as a whole. Both these opposite attitudes contain some truth; together they reflect a feeling about the powerful and mysterious nature of group forces, and an acknowledgment that groups contain potentialities for both benefit and harm to their individual members.

The conduct of individuals can be explained in terms of ambivalence, i.e. in terms of opposing and simultaneously operating loves and hates. We find comparable forces operating at a group level, and these forces are represented by the tendencies of the group to continue, i.e. its coherence, and the tendencies of the group to break up, i.e. its disruptiveness. *The simultaneously operating coherence and disruptiveness constitute the ambivalence of the group.* It may well be that only one aspect of this "group ambivalence" will find expression at any one moment, but in order to understand the behaviour of the group, the other component must be assumed to exist in an undisclosed form.

The first problem facing the group is to survive, just as the last problem is to disband. Groups survive when their opposing tendencies can be reconciled. They also survive when they are able to provide sufficient satisfaction for the needs of each of their members so that the wish to belong is strong enough to overcome the wish to be separate.

Thus, when we consider what happened at any particular group meeting, and wonder why events followed the course that they did, we need to take into account the following factors :

1. The overt purpose and structure of the group.
2. The problems and needs that each individual member brings into the group, and which he attempts to solve and satisfy through the group.
3. The conflict that each member experiences about belonging to the group. If his needs are insufficiently satisfied, his wish to break away may become stronger· than his wish to remain.
4. The totality which adds up to a basic group problem, and which cannot be equated with the problem of any one individual member but belongs in some way to them all. The problem is that of the group's survival through the promotion of its cohesiveness and the containment of its disruptiveness. It is within this basic problem that the group processes operate.

A final illustration can be provided from the record of a group consisting of mothers of young, mentally handicapped children, who met together every week with a social worker.

This is an example of one of the types of group that will be considered in detail in a later chapter. The aim of the group meetings was to help the mothers in relationship to their children, and the discussion, though focused upon the children, was otherwise free and unstructured. In the first few meetings, the mothers all related anecdotes about the behaviour of their subnormal children, and a marked uniformity in opinions and attitudes was shown. When one mother described the behaviour of her child at table or at bedtime, one or two of the other mothers would join in eagerly, claiming that their children behaved in exactly the same way. Inconsistencies and contradictions soon became apparent, and it appeared that the mothers were less concerned with giving accurate descriptions of their children's behaviour than with maintaining unanimity at all costs. Only one mother, at the second meeting of the group, described her child as being different, and she received exaggerated sympathy from the others. She did not attend the next meeting, and the group immediately referred to her and discussed her problems at length, dwelling on the abnormality of her child's behaviour, and criticising the ways in which she handled him.

These were women who found it difficult, because of their children's handicaps, to take part in normal corporate activities, and they all, to some degree, felt painfully different from mothers in general. Their behaviour demonstrated the strength of their wish to be in a group where they could share freely and did not have to feel exceptional. But it also indicated the strength of the disruptive forces threatening the group. Side by side with the wish to belong to the group were strong competitive and hostile feelings which the group situation tended to intensify. Most of these mothers were prepared to fight to obtain special provision for their children, and were reluctant to have them classified with other "subnormals". Not all the mothers, of course, experienced these negative feelings to an equal extent. But the conflict between disruptive and cohesive forces posed an immediate problem, and led to the adoption of a group solution in which most participated actively and a few acquiesced. The one mother who refused to acquiesce left the group.

It was the strength of these two opposing drives, to belong and to be separate, that was responsible for the establishment of this artificial uniformity. This behaviour of the group members ensured that the group (minus the one who left) could continue to exist over the early sessions. It was not until the group was more securely established, and relationships among the mothers, and between the mothers and the social worker, were stronger than this restricting solution could be gradually abandoned and some tolerant expression of separate feelings could be allowed.

CHAPTER 3

The Group Situation

IMAGINE a small number of people coming together regularly, perhaps at weekly intervals, and spending about an hour and a half in each other's company. They meet as equals, and they sit in a circle and talk together. There is a leader, with special knowledge and skills, who is there to help them. He seems to exercise less direct control over the proceedings than one normally expects from a leader, and may even appear to follow rather than lead. It is not a business or committee meeting that has brought these people together, since there is no agenda, no chairman, no reference to any external task. It is not a social or recreational occasion, since there appears to be a serious purpose. No systematic instruction is given, so the purpose does not seem to be formal education. There is no discernible ambition to bring about changes in the wider community, so it is not a political meeting. There is no reference to supernatural force, moral code, creed, or body of doctrine, so it is not in any sense a religious assembly. The focus is upon what goes on in the group, the dynamic inter-changes, the contributions of members and of leader, and on this alone. Whatever it is that the members are seeking, it seems to be contained here.

Such a meeting as this could be taking place in any one of a variety of different settings. It could be in a private consult-ing room, hospital, clinic, social work agency, prison, school, or university. The members could be patients, inmates of an institution, members of a youth club, prisoners, or professional students of such disciplines as medicine, psychology, social work, teaching, or nursing. The leader could belong to any one of a number of different professions, including those listed above, each with its own techniques and its own distinct body of professional knowledge. Thus the groups may vary considerably in their settings, in their compositions, and in the disciplines of their leaders. They may also differ widely in their purposes and in their proceedings, in what the individual members hope to gain and in what the leader attempts to contribute.

These are the groups that form the subject of this book. Their diversity will be considered in later chapters, when an attempt will be made to classify them under three main headings. For the present, we are concerned with their general characteristics, and with certain features which they have in common and which set them apart from all other groups.

The first common feature we find is in the purpose that has brought the members of these groups together. Each member has come to his group because he is dissatisfied, at some level or in some degree, with his present situation. It may be a dissatisfaction with the whole of his present life, or with one small part of it; it may be severe or slight; he may be seeking relief from a severe mental illness, looking for help with some family difficulty, or seeking to ease the transition from one stage of life to another; or he may be wishing to extend the range of certain professional skills. But whatever the problems and dissatisfactions of individual members, or whatever new satisfactions are being sought, they all have this in common : each of them is concerned with relationships between people. It is in this area that the dissatisfactions are expressed, and it is also in this area that the remedies are being sought.

We know that we cannot carry on life in isolation from our fellows, and that it is on the quality of the relationships that we make with other people that so much of our happiness and success depends. Through these relationships we either meet, or fail to meet, most of our basic needs. They are not only central to our intimate, personal lives, but they also affect every activity in which we have contact with other people, at home, at work, and at play, and they play a part in the use of most professional skills. There are professions in which the contribution made by skill and sensitivity in interpersonal relationships is explicitly recognised. "The doctor–patient relationship" and "the casework relationship" are discussed as professional techniques, and they have their counterparts in other disciplines and other occupations. Every relationship between two people is a two-way process to which both contribute, and any professional practice concerned with living beings in face-to-face situations may require from the worker a deeper understanding of his own behaviour as well as of the behaviour of others. In this way such work differs from work dealing with inanimate objects, which alone can be "objective". Such deeper understanding is not easy to acquire, and it cannot be achieved by an intellectual process alone. It may sometimes be sought, as may the relief of mental illness, and the resolution of personal problems, through participation of the activities of a group.

The members of all these groups, with their different motivations and different degrees of commitment, are seeking to improve the quality of the relationships which they make with other people, to learn to recognise the contribution they themselves make to every personal relationship in which they are involved, and to take responsibility for that contribution. To this end they are prepared, in the groups they have joined, to expose themselves to new situations which contain the possibility of personal charge. This brings us to a further point in common : the aims of all our groups include the promotion of a degree of change in their individual members. This change is not something that takes place through the influence of any external factor, nor is it change in some determined direction. The members of the group are not converted, nor indoctrinated, nor, for this purpose, should they be instructed. The agent of change is participation in the group itself, and in its processes, operating under exceptional and disciplined conditions. Though all groups have their dynamics, and there are potentialities for change, growth, and development in every human encounter, we are considering very particular situations in which an attempt is made to be aware of these potentialities and to influence them.

Change in itself may be frightening. It leads to something not yet experienced, and the thought of this may be painful. Change is not necessarily beneficial, and even where it is beneficial it involves the surrender of some present good. We tend to spend much of our energy trying to avoid change, endeavouring to maintain an existing situation because we fear that any alteration might involve loss rather than gain. So in every individual, and in every group of individuals, there are forces that resist change. Singly and together, we have our defences. We possess certain beliefs that we do not wish to be questioned; we have standards that we like to assume are self-evident. Even when we are conscious of certain inadequacies and failings in ourselves, we may not be prepared to have them brought to the attention of others. We try to present ourselves to the world in a favourable light, concealing our less acceptable side, pretending that all is well. It is not easy for us to abandon this pretence, and, moreover, any attempt to do so is likely to be discouraged by others who will feel it as a threat to their own security. The frankness of one person is a challenge to the concealments of everyone else, and those who speak plainly of their own shortcomings may, in fact, expose others more than themselves.

For many of us, it is hard openly to acknowledge a need, for we fear that, if the need is known, it may be ignored, and then our burden would be doubled. It is hard to acknowledge ignorance and incompetence, for we fear contempt and loss of esteem. We are afraid that others may take advantage of any weaknesses that we may reveal. Thus our insecurity makes us assume positions that are hard to relinquish, and that make change unlikely. Others of us, on the other hand, may cling to our weaknesses as an entitlement to consideration that we are reluctant to surrender, fearing any change that might bring greater challenges and greater demands.

At another level altogether, there are aspects of ourselves that we struggle to conceal not only from our associates but even from our own conscious selves. These aspects may threaten not only our standing with others but our very existence. We are afraid that any slackening in our self-control could release primitive impulses of which we are only dimly aware, and that these impulses might overwhelm us, even to the point of disintegration and madness.

We have seen that unstructured group situations are felt to be frightening. They contain a danger that too much will be revealed. The less structure there is in a group, the less are we able to hide ourselves in stereotyped roles, and the less predictable will be our own behaviour and that of the others. Less, too, will be the restrictions on the free play of group forces, which are also feared. But the group situations in which we customarily find ourselves in our day-to-day lives have much of their challenge removed through rules and regulations, social conventions and agreed standards of behaviour. These preserve our accustomed roles, and protect us from unexpected encounters and embarrassing revelations.

The group that are the subject of this study differ from these other groups in a fundamental way. If the members are ready to expose themselves to the possibility of change, they must also be ready to abandon some part of their defences, to relinquish some part of their controls, to reveal more of their weaknesses, and to be more honest both with themselves and with others. Some of the conventions of social intercourse, with which they would normally protect themselves, must be abandoned. It has to be learned that there is no safety in numbers.

Such changes in behaviour do not come about merely by willing them. The ways in which we habitually react are not usually within our conscious control. If members of a group are going to be able to behave in a different way, then they must feel that they are in a different situation; if they are to modify the defences they use in order to feel secure, then alternative sources of security have to be provided. The margin of safety has to be extended. This will not happen all at once, and the extra security of the group will have to be built up by degrees, as the members test out and thus extend the permitted limits. They will be helped in this by the knowledge that they all have similar purposes, and by the gradual sharing of confidences and experiences. But whatever may happen in the group to help or hinder the development of this process, the safety of the group and of individual members is ultimately the responsibility of the group leader. It is part of his function to ensure that free exchanges can take place without danger, that no one is subjected to more stress than he can tolerate, and that the group does not break up until it has accomplished its purpose. No leader can always expect to be completely successful in this.

It is also the leader's responsibility to see that the aims of the group are observed. These aims set bounds and limits to the proceedings, and any self-exposure should not overstep the limits set by the group's particular aim. Each member has to relinquish some part of his normal controls, and, in doing so, he vests these controls in the leader. Removing one of his outer garments, he relies on the leader to ensure that the room is kept warm enough for his body heat to be maintained. He also relies on the leader to prevent him from taking off so many clothes that he will either catch cold or be improperly exposed.

In every one of these groups, an implicit bargain is made between each group member and the leader. Within the terms of reference determined by the aim of the group, the leader guarantees that the difficulties can be discussed and feelings revealed in safety. Outside the terms of reference, he guarantees that privacy will be respected. In some groups, the terms of reference will be drawn widely, and in some they will be drawn narrowly. In each situation, the group member will only be prepared to expose himself to the extent that he has confidence in the power of the leader to guarantee his safety when conditions in the group itself cannot do so. This confidence may be helped initially by the acknowledged position of the leader, but it depends in the longer run upon his skill in this role.

The leader may not be required to make any direct interventions. Sufficient conditions of safety at each stage may come to be provided by the group itself as it develops and matures. Through the operation of group processes, a broad, tacit, consensus of opinion can be expected to develop about the behaviour of individuals in the group, the honouring of confidences, the tolerance of divergencies, the level of reciprocal disclosures. The leader will not wish to interfere with the free development of such a consensus, which, though constantly shifting, will be far more effective than any ruling of his would be. However, his presence is still necessary as the ultimate guarantor. His very presence will be a reassurance when the strength and cohesiveness of the group seem insufficient.

Some members of a group will always be more vulnerable than others, and sensitivity in different situations will vary. Sometimes one member will introduce a topic, make comments, or ask questions, for which others in the group are not ready and which they find too disturbing. For various reasons, and in various ways, individual members may find themselves isolated and criticised. The result of all this may be one or more members who are unable to participate or who may even leave the group. The disruptive forces in the group, of which all are afraid, will need to find some expression; but if they are expressed too early, before sufficient cohesion has developed to contain them, they may lead to the group's disintegration. In any of the groups we are considering, the leader may be required to intervene to protect a particular member, or to protect the group as a whole; to increase the safety of one of them or of all of them; and to help the group to develop sufficient strength and cohesiveness for its purpose. He may also have to intervene to see that any necessary limits are observed, and that privacy of members outside these limits is respected. In this way he fulfills his side of the bargain.

This concept of a bargain between group member and group leader, "implicit" because it can seldom be explicitly formulated at the outset, plays an important part in our argument. It is included in the concept of the "mandate" which is given by the party seeking personal help to the party offering it and which must not be exceeded. This concept has been questioned.[1] It has been argued, in relation to social work, that the client of the social worker is rarely in any position to appreciate the nature and the limitations of the help he is being offered, or to forecast what is going to be demanded of him, and that therefore it is an act of self-deception for social workers to speak as if there were a contract freely entered into by both parties. By the same argument, the individual who joins any of the groups we are considering may well have no clear and accurate idea of what will be involved, but this does not mean that he is agreeing to participate in an unlimited process. He joins a group for some particular purpose, and he expects that the leader will do all he can to see that this purpose, and none other, is achieved. In this sense he empowers the leader to act in certain ways; if he does not understand what these ways are, he is able to support the uncertainty because of his belief that the leader understands them. The fact that group members and group leaders are embarking upon a joint task of uncertain direction and outcome makes it all the more important that its ultimate aims and limits should be understood and respected by the leaders who must take responsibility for them. The consent of the members may often initially be based upon an act of faith, but it is ratified by their increasing involvement

[1] Paul Halmos, *The Faith of the Counsellors*, Constable, 1965.

in the groups which they have joined. The leaders are fully committed at the beginning, but the members may extend the area of their commitment gradually. For them, the bargain is not a static one but a living experience which makes possible the organic growth and development of the group as a whole.

CHAPTER 4

Distinguishing the Three Systems

AT THIS point it is necessary to make some preliminary distinctions among all these groups which, so far, have been described together, but which in fact differ considerably in their aims and in the methods used to realise these aims. We proposed to divide these groups into three categories, which we shall call Group Psychotherapy, Group Counselling, and Group Discussion. We attempt to base these distinctions upon a consideration of what actually takes place in these groups, and not upon a consideration of the designation of the leader, the status of the members, nor the nature of the setting, nor even upon the avowed purpose of the meeting. These distinctions are made in order to provide a framework which will help to differentiate other group work methods from Group Psychotherapy, to give these other methods a firmer conceptual basis, and to facilitate teaching and communication in this area. A clearer understanding about the use of terms in this field is badly needed. Thus in the report of the Home Office Research Unit entitled *A Survey of Group Work in the Probation Service*, the authors deliberately avoid using such precise terms because they consider that "at our present stage in understanding what takes place in these groups there does not appear to be a clear-cut distinction between the methods". They add the warning that "attaching a label to a type of treatment can give a misleading impression of a unified body of theory and treatment practice, which may not exist". We heed the warning, and our framework is offered as a contribution to the remedying of this deficiency.

Group Discussion, Group Counselling, and Group Psychotherapy, all share the area in common that was outlined in the last chapter. They all have aims which include the promotion of a degree of personal change in each member; each member is prepared to expose himself to change to a greater extent than he would do in other situations, and each member relies on a leader with special skills to be the ultimate guarantor that it is safe to do so. Any change that takes place in individual members comes about solely through participation in the processes taking place within the group itself. The differences are to be found in the aim of the groups; in the nature, degree, and purpose, of the change that is sought; in the role played by the group leader; and in the psychological level of depth and particularity at which each group operates. The three methods have an additional point in common in the part derivation of their theoretical bases from dynamic theories of group psychology, but each also has its own separate roots in a different individual helping process.

Group Psychotherapy will be considered first, since it is from here that much of the theory of group behaviour common to all three systems is derived. Group Psychotherapy has its counterpart in individual psychotherapy. In the latter, the aim is to bring about a radical and permanent change in the personality of the "patient". The setting is traditionally a medical one; the psychotherapist will either have a medical qualification himself or be working under the supervision of somebody who has. The patient is prepared, at any rate theoretically, to reveal his most private thoughts and phantasies, however painful this may be, holding nothing back; and he relies on the psychotherapist to protect him from the feared and real consequences of such a surrender of his defences.

There are a number of different schools of psychotherapy, but, for the most part, use is made of the concept of transference. The psychotherapist will base his work upon the interpretation of the transference relationship, going back to the deeply unconscious feelings which the infant had for his original love objects, and which are currently transferred into the therapist–patient relationship. Though the patient may have sought help on account of some particular difficulty, the therapist will focus upon the person, and not upon the problem, as he tries to effect a total change. His concern is with the patient's inner world, and with this alone.

We are considering a notional and, perhaps, idealised model of psychotherapy in order to point the contrast between the different systems. For our purpose we are confining the term "psychotherapy" to a specific process within a precise framework of patient and psychotherapist with an implied contract to devote themselves to the purpose of the treatment. The principles of psychoanalytic psychotherapy have penetrated in varying degrees into the general culture and into the practice of social work, education, and other professional frameworks. In this way psychotherapeutic principles have enlarged the scope and deepened the effect of the practice of other caring professions. None of these extensions is included in our consideration of psychotherapy; we are treating it as a procedure confined to the consulting room.

Much of the above, which is derived from the consideration of individual psychotherapy, also applied to Group Psychotherapy. The declared aim of Group Psychotherapy is to effect a significant change in the personality of each member of the group. As with individual psychotherapy, normal social rules are suspended, and each member of the group is expected to reveal his thoughts and feelings with complete freedom, on the understanding that the psychotherapist will be able to maintain the safety of the group and protect each member from any adverse consequences. The transference is now a multidimensional one, and at any one time a wider range of unconscious attitudes are brought into the treatment situation. The role that the group psychotherapist plays will depend upon his theoretical framework, and his conception of the nature of the group processes; he may focus upon the behaviour of the individual in the group or, at the other end of a continuum, he may confine his interventions to effect only those processes which take place within the group as a whole.

Compared with Group Psychotherapy, Group Counselling has a more definite and directed aim. It is concerned with relieving particular problems and with modifying specific situations. To this end it may be necessary to bring about changes in some attitudes and relationships, but fundamental changes in the structure of personality are not specifically sought. Group Counselling may be carried out by members of different disciplines, and is not a technique exclusive to any one profession, but for its individual counterpart one must look to the one-to-one casework relationship which has been developed by social workers.

Social caseworkers are employed within specialist agencies, and have definite terms of reference. A client will be referred to a particular agency because his particular problem falls within its terms of reference. Although the caseworker will need to make a complete assessment of the situation in which the client finds himself, and may try to bring about a general improvement in his circumstances and in his system of personal relationships, the caseworker never loses sight of the original problem for which the client sought help. The client is expected to talk frankly about his problem, and he expects that it will be safe for him to do so, but there is no expectation that he is to reveal himself completely and hold nothing back. Should the client choose to do so, the caseworker must handle the situation within the limits determined by his training and experience, making such use of the client's contribution as he can within the particular framework set by his agency. He needs to be aware that there are dangers in extending the treatment process to include a form of psychotherapy which has not been sanctioned, and in which he is not trained.

The caseworker makes use of the relationship which he

establishes with his client, and this relationship furnishes the context in which other forms of help may be offered, material as well as psychological. He needs to be aware of the transference, but even though he may recognise it, he does not need to interpret it in the way that a psychotherapist does. His training as well as his terms of reference have got other aims in areas in which, conversely, a psychotherapist would be ill equipped and ill at lease. He may need to demonstrate how a client is carrying over attitudes and feelings from the past into the present, but the attitudes and feelings will be conscious or near-conscious ones; and they will be the ones that affect the practical issues in the client's life.

Compared with the psychotherapist, the caseworker has more freedom to select and set limits to his treatment aims and to the themes that are to be discussed. Although he may have to limit his focus to specific problems, he can select from a range of different helping techniques, and he does not have to avoid behaviour that might conceivably interfere with the untrammelled development of the transference relationship.

Group Counselling derives from casework, and its counterpart is found in some particular aspects of the casework process with the individual. But it cannot be tailored to meet individual needs in the way that casework can, nor can it include such a wide range of individual helping methods. Members of a counselling group will share some common problem or situation which provides a point of focus and to which everything that takes place in the group needs to be related. It is the task of the group counseller to maintain this focus and to make the links that establish these relationships. Thus the proceedings of the group, and the interactions between all the group members, the contributions and the responses of each individual, are all made to play their part in the problem-solving process. The group counsellor may play an unobtrusive part in the proceedings, keeping his own personality in the background, and in this respect his behaviour may resemble that of a group psychotherapist; on the other hand, the needs of individual members and of the total group may require him to play a more active role, and make a positive and direct use of his relationship with them. Again, there is a counterpart in the different uses that the caseworker in an individual setting may make of his relationship with his client.

Group Discussion, in its turn, differs from Group Psycho-therapy and Group Counselling in having an aim that is primarily educational. The focus of the group work is not upon particular difficulties of personality or of relationships, or upon specific problems, but upon topics that are presented for development and elucidation. The processes that take place in the group are used to develop and elucidate the topics, and thus they become an educational tool.

One important application of Group Discussion is as a means of helping workers in the field of human relations to increase their insights and skills. The application has a counter-part in the individual supervision or consultation process, in which a student or junior worker will bring problems for discussion with a supervisor. This is a form of learning which cannot take place through intellectual means alone; the problems that the student encounters in his work, and the specific difficulties, are likely to be linked to factors in his own personality, and their resolution will largely depend upon the growth of his own self-awareness. However, his relationship with his supervisor is not a therapeutic nor a casework one. This means that the supervisor has no sanction to intervene in the student's personal problems and should seek no direct knowledge of them. Both parties should understand this, and both should know that the other understands it. Details of the student's behaviour on the job and the relationships that he makes with others in the course of his work may have to be discussed, but the supervisor will make no direct links between them and any other aspects of the student's life of which he may have knowledge. A student capable of personal growth may be able to make use of the opportunity to do this for himself.

In practice, some information about the student's personal history may be disclosed and cannot be thrust aside. The supervisor has to make a response to such disclosures, distinguishing this response from his other activities as a supervisor, and placing it outside the narrow professional framework within which he and his student have their disciplined and functional relationship. Even though the supervisor's responses are designed to be helpful, the occasion is not converted into a therapeutic encounter. If more than this is needed, the student should be referred elsewhere for casework or therapy on a formal basis, in which he would have the right to disengage himself should he so desire.

Group Discussion, like consultation or supervision, can be used for the development of professional skills and understanding, but the method is more indirect, and the focus more upon the general than upon the particular. The topics that are discussed are concerned with human and interpersonal behaviour, so that the behaviour that takes place in the group cannot be ignored but will be used to illustrate and to test the validity of some of the concepts put forward. Members of the discussion group will expect the leader to refrain from intruding into their personal lives, and to prevent others from doing so. They expect to be able to expose their work problems without encountering personal criticism or ridicule, and in the knowledge that the other members are prepared to do likewise. In discussion, members will necessarily reveal the nature of their defences and the areas in which they feel less secure, and they will need confidence to reveal these areas. The leader may comment, as in individual supervision, on details of particular cases or individual professional difficulties described by members, or he may concentrate his comments on matters involving the group as a whole. He will need the skill to make use of the contributions of the less confident, and to construct a framework in which the contributions of all can be included. He will need to protect the vulnerable, and is more likely to repair defences than to interpret their nature.

However, the Group Discussion leader has more scope than the consultant or supervisor in an individual situation to use interpretation of the immediate situation as one of his techniques. Attention can be drawn to a group process without any personal intrusion, whereas a supervisor with one student would have to be much more circumspect in commenting on the current relationship between the two of them.

Sometimes Group Discussion is used for education about group work itself, in any of its forms. Through participation in such a situation, with the help of the group leader, the members will hope to develop their awareness of the group processes. The topic on which such a group is focused is group behaviour, which must include the behaviour of this particular group. The leader needs to be able to make appropriate use of the example that the behaviour of this group supplies, and to help members to increase their insight and understanding, but at the same time avoid implicit or explicit references to personal behaviour that is not sanctioned.

So far, we have been looking at Group Discussion as a means of professional education. The method can be used for other purposes and in other settings. There are, for example, the classes in human relationships that are provided in many schools and youth clubs; and there are the Marriage Preparation courses for engaged couples that are part of the activity of the Marriage Guidance Council. Though these groups may differ markedly in many significant respects, such as their homogeneity, the level of sophistication of the members, and the ability of the members to withstand stress, the same basic principles apply to them all. The focus in all these groups is upon topics. The leader helps the members to respond freely to the topic. The leader constructs a framework by relating together all the individual contributions. The privacy of the individual is respected.

No mention has yet been made of Activity Groups. These are groups in which the members come together in the first instance to take part in some shared activity such as acting, painting, boat building, or photography, and in which the leader attempts to make use of the occasion provided, and the group situation, to help members in other ways. Activity groups are found in such settings as mental hospitals, prisons, special schools, and probation offices. Much of what has been said applies to these groups also; they too have their dynamics, and a leader able to recognise and work with the group processes may significantly influence the development of these groups and the progress of individual members. Successful participation in any group activity, no matter what that activity may be, can bring considerable benefits for the individual. It provides a positive experience in human relationships, helping to promote the growth of capacities which can be transferred to relationships in other settings, and helping to develop qualities such as generosity, tolerance, and the ability to share. All groups, not excluding psychotherapeutic ones, derive no small part of their benefit from the opportunity which they provide to participate successfully in a social activity.

Although we wish to recognise the existence and the importance of activity groups, we propose to confine any detailed consideration to groups whose main business is carried on through verbal communication.

The terms that are used to designate the three group work systems, Group Psychotherapy, Group Counselling, and Group Discussion, are all in common usage, but there is little consistency in their use, and they normally convey little clear information about the treatment or educational process actually taking place in the groups they are used to describe.

The imprecise use of language is one difficulty. Another is caused by the fact that some concepts and techniques are shared by all three of our systems, and this overlap sometimes gives an impression that there is only one basic group process which can be applied at different levels of depth and intensity in different circumstances. This impression is based upon a failure to appreciate the importance of the differences in the

aims of different groups, and also the differences in what ha
been sanctioned. These are decisive factors which require t(
be clearly formulated at the outset, as they provide the contex
which determines what techniques are appropriate.

A number of additional factors add to the current confusion
The following have all played their part.

Group Psychotherapy is the only one of the three grou
systems we are considering in which progress has been mad
towards establishing a firm conceptual basis, or which ca
make claim to be regarded as a scientific discipline. It is fron
Group Psycholtherapy that the knowledge of group dynamic
necessary to all group workers is derived. Social workers wh
wish to work with groups are frequently, and by their ow
choice, trained and supervised by group psychotherapists. It i
not surprising that social workers often appear unable, o
unwilling, to consider their work as belonging to a separat
system, but look on it rather as a diluted and attenuated forr
of psychotherapy, and see advance in skill in terms of an eve
closer approximation to the work described by group psychc
therapists. While usually disclaiming use of the actual terr
Group Psychotherapy, they do their best to adopt the methoc
and the terminology.

Social workers may disclaim the term, but others do no
The difference between the three systems is further obscure
when the term psychotherapy is treated as medical propert
and "Group Psychotherapy" is used to indicate that the leade
of the group has a medical qualification, and tells us nothin
about the purpose of the group or what is taking place in i
Sometimes the qualifying adjective "limited" or "superficia
is added, and this may or may not be a disclaimer and indica
that the leader is untrained in both group work and in psychc
therapy. It is unfortunate if group leaders who have a medic
qualification feel precluded from using an appropriate termi
ology to describe what they are doing only because the
cannot make use of terms which they associate with the wo
of other disciplines.

Members of many different disciplines are called upon to lead discussion groups. There is not always sufficient recognition of the fact that Group Discussion is a separate technique, and that competence in it is not automatically conferred by training or experience in Group Counselling or Group Psychotherapy. Discussion groups have on occasions been turned into psychotherapeutic groups simply because psychotherapy has been the only technique that the leader has had at his disposal.

A group work project is sometimes undertaken without any prior formulation of aims and terms of references, or appreciation that this is needed. This may be the result of a belief that therapeutic forces reside in the group itself, and that bringing people together is in itself a therapeutic act. This seems to be a half-truth. A group contains both therapeutic and anti-therapeutic potential, and the group forces may help or harm the individual. Group work can always be hazardous, and particularly so if it is unfocused and undirected.

In order to provide a framework, and a basis for further discussion, we have put our emphasis upon the separateness of the different systems, and stressed their differences. We may have implied the existence of a uniformity within these differences, of definite boundaries and distinctions, which do not exist in practice. In fact, not only do all the groups we are considering share many concepts and techniques, but there are also considerable areas of overlap, and the boundaries often seem blurred rather than clear-cut. There are different schools of Group Psychotherapy, differing in their theoretical basis and in their techniques. The members of some psychotherapeutic groups may be selected on the basis of some problem, such as drug addiction, which they all share. Group counsellors define different aims in different groups, and vary in the use they make of interpretative techniques and of their own relationship with the group; some may widen their focus to include more aspects of their clients' past and present experience. Group Discussion can be used to serve different ends, and adjusted to meet the needs of different groups which may be very varied in terms of age, education, and degree of personal commitment. Some discussion groups may focus upon a topic which contains personal and intimate preoccupations of its members which cannot remain unexpressed.

The proceedings of every group will be influenced not only by the particular discipline to which the leader belongs, and his particular theoretical orientation, but also by his own leadership style, his interests and experience, his personal make-up, and even his psychopathology. This influence cannot be considered an improper one, for group leadership is not a mechanical skill; rather, it is a process in which the spontaneous use of the leader's personality plays an important part. There is much that can be learnt, a disciplined framework and a theoretical base are essential, but within this framework and upon this base each group leader develops his own personal style of leadership and gives his group something that no one else could give.

The context of the group, its aim, its focus, and its sanctions, must never be forgotten. The way in which the role of the leader in each of the three systems needs to be related to the purpose of the group is illustrated in the following example : it deals with a situation that must be familiar to all group workers. Let us suppose that a new group assembles and that at the first few meetings a predominant feeling in the group is anxiety at being in a new and uncharted situation. Although they react in different ways, all the members share in this group tension and in the efforts that are made to deal with it. Typically, they turn to the group leader and put pressure on him to take a more active part and to give more structure to the proceedings.

To a group psychotherapist, this tension provides the very material with which he works. He will do nothing to lessen it in order to allow the group members to feel more comfortable. On the contrary, he will allow it to develop until it becomes expressed and resolved, or until he considers it appropriate to make an interpretation or other intervention, not primarily to lower the tension but rather to permit further development. Painful experiences are necessary to psychotherapeutic progress, and members of such a group must be prepared to face some discomfort.

If a similar tension developed in a counselling group, it would be dealt with in a different way. Here there is no sanction, in the bargain between leader and members, for the same level of discomfort, and outside a psychotherapeutic framework it would be likely to have a disruptive effect, perhaps even leading to the break-up of the group. In a counselling group, there is not the same need to foster free communication and the unhampered growth of transference relationships, so the leader has a wider choice of approaches, and is free to play a more active part himself. He will decide what to do in the light of the particular aim that has been defined for the group, and of the needs of its members. It might be appropriate for him to accede to the wishes of the group for the time being, and to play the more active part that they wish. For example, in a counselling group of ex-mental hospital patients, a common problem for all the members might be difficulty in leaving the ordered regime of a paternalistic institution. Stress in the group will involve stress on individual members, and such members may, temporarily or permanently, have both a limited capacity to tolerate stress and a need to form a dependent relationship with the group leader. Thus the leader will adjust his behaviour to the particular needs of this group. Alternatively, or in addition, to such a use of his relationship with the group, he might make an interpretation or a comparison. He might do this by commenting on what is taking place in the group and linking it to the problem which provides the group's focus, in this instance the problems of adjustment to life outside the hospital. The relationships which are finding expression within the present group could be compared by the leader

with the new relationships that individual members have ye
to make outside the hospital.

In Group Discussion the leader would have to handl
the tension in relation to some aspect of the group's topic
using it, if he can, to clarify and stimulate, avoiding a degre
of stress that would expose the inadequacies of the mos
vulnerable. Such a situation would be very relevant to th
theme of groups who are concerned with discussing problem
of dependency; dependency in relationships between parent
and children, in marriage relationships, or in relationship
between professional workers and patients or clients. It might
in fact, be an advantage to such groups to experience, an
then to discuss, a situation in which dependency is both sough
and denied. Although, in Group Discussion, less stress o
individuals is sanctioned, the capacity of the group and o
individual members to tolerate new and experimental situation
may be greater. The behaviour of the group as a whole ma
be used by the leader to illustrate the theme, but no attentio
will be paid to individual personal problems that may b
revealed in the course of the exercise.

So each of the three leaders in the three different grou
systems may be confronted with a very similar situation i
his group. Each will be required to respond to this situatio
in some way. In their responses, all the three leaders use a
understanding of the dynamic processes which take place i
all groups, and all three look beyond the individual member
to the group as a whole, but each one handles a comparabl
situation in a different way because he relates his respons
to the aims of the group, and he gives regard to what ha
been sanctioned.

CHAPTER 5

Group Psychotherapy

THE practice of bringing small numbers of patients together to share their psychotherapeutic sessions may have been undertaken by a few pioneers even before the First World War, but it is only since 1945 that it has been practised on any large scale. It is now a familiar and accepted part of the psychiatric scene. The development of theory has followed upon practice, in the same way that psychoanalytic theory did not become formulated until Freud had used the psychoanalytic method for the treatment of patients. But there is no single theory of group psychotherapy as such; instead we have a bewildering variety of different theoretical systems, some differing radically from each other, and some separated more by degrees of emphasis. The present position of group psychotherapy could be compared with the early days of psychoanalysis, when Freud's followers were all laying their separate claims to new discoveries and new formulations. Today, there is a similar wealth in the contributions of group psychotherapists, and, as techniques become more refined, and are used more precisely, so the terminology becomes more complicated. The outstanding group psychotherapists have their adherents, sharing common assumptions about group dynamics and about processes that are considered to be therapeutic, but it would be premature to speak as if coherent schools of thought existed. It is possible for the group psychotherapist in training to become familiar with, and to make use of, a wide range of different theories.

51

In order to study these different theories, it is important to be able to classify them in some way. One way in which they differ is in the importance that is attached to any single event taking place in the group, and the context or perspective in which that event is placed. Thus, a single event taking place in a group can be seen as the product of one particular group member, as the product of the interaction between two or more group members, or as the product or the sum of all the interactions taking place.

The first viewpoint is represented in theories which treat activity taking place at an intra-personal level, within the individual, as the most relevant and significant. Here the therapist makes use of a model drawn from the two-person situation of individual psychoanalysis. He sets out to treat the individual within a group setting and conducts something resembling psychoanalysis in public with a participating audience. Some exponents of this method claim that it is an improvement on individual psychoanalysis because the support that each member derives from being a member of a group increases his tolerance of anxiety and enables deeper levels to be reached more quickly. Slavson, Locke, and Schwartz are the best-known group psychotherapists who take this position.

Others have placed their main emphasis upon a conceptualisation of events at an interpersonal level, i.e. as transactions taking place between more than one individual, and the products of dynamic interpersonal relationships. An example is the games that Berne has uncovered.

A third point of departure is to regard each group event as being determined or influenced by all other happenings in the group, and by the complete network of relationships that includes all members. Thus each event has, in addition to its significance for individuals, a significance at a transpersonal or group level, and the sum of all the intra- and inter-personal transactions has a meaning which can only be understood by considering the group as a whole. The total group situation always has to be taken into account.

This last viewpoint is associated with Bion, Foulkes, Ezriel, and Stock Whitaker and Lieberman. It is also our own viewpoint, which we have already indicated, and which is fundamental to this book.

It is not our aim to attempt a comprehensive description of Group Psychotherapy, however brief. The purpose of this chapter is more limited. We propose, firstly, to refer briefly to four selected theories of group behaviour; these are theories which, though derived from the practice of group psychotherapy, have an application that extends beyond its boundaries and are very relevant to our formulation. These theories are psychoanalytically orientated and they also focus upon the behaviour of the group as a whole; they differ at many points, however, and at times make use of rather different terminologies. They are concerned with finding answers to the questions that have been considered in the preceding chapters of this book, i.e. "What forces determine a group's behaviour?", "How does each individual contribute to these group forces?", and "What is the impact of these forces on the individual?" These questions are important, not only to group psychotherapists, but also to others, including those who wish to utilise group methods for counselling and discussion. Anyone embarking on group work of any kind, including therapy, counselling, and discussion, must start from some particular viewpoint and must have hypotheses about group behaviour, a framework, and a vocabulary. Though the data for developing group theories may be available in all groups, it is in psychotherapeutic groups that they are most accessible and have been most intensively studied, and hence it is to group psychotherapists that we owe the dynamic concepts that make the discussion of these questions possible.

Our second aim in this chapter on Group Psychotherapy is to contribute to the development of a theoretical basis for Group Counselling and Group Discussion by indicating where the boundaries of the three systems may be drawn. For this purpose it is necessary to postulate a model "Group Psychotherapy", belonging to all schools and likely to be recognised by none, and to attribute to it certain features which we believe belong essentially to Group Psychotherapy and not to Group Counselling nor to Group Discussion.

We shall first consider the four different approaches to Group Psychotherapy at their point of greatest abstraction, where they deal with group events at a transpersonal level and offer concepts which make it possible to comprehend the inter-relatedness of all events taking place in a group, and the existence of a total pattern of behaviour which includes but transcends the individual members.

We do not attempt to do justice to these theories; their importance in this book is apparent. Those with a serious interest in group work as part of a therapeutic system will need to turn to the works of their originators (see Bibliography).

The psychoanalytic approach is characterised by the belief that every piece of human behaviour has meaning at two levels, the manifest and the latent, the conscious and the unconscious; there is the everyday level of conscious response to the perceived realities of the situation in which the individual finds himself, and there is the level at which behaviour can only be comprehended in terms of a response to unconscious drives and basic emotional needs. Although it is a mistake to think that psychoanalytic concepts derived from the study of individuals can be applied directly to groups, the concept of conscious and unconscious levels is fundamental to both fields. The two levels are applied to the behaviour of groups at a transpersonal level by Bion. In his theoretical system Bion describes the *Work Group*, which corresponds in many ways to the Freudian Ego and which contains the rational, conscious, orderly aspect of the group's behaviour. This is the level which we all know. At this level members of a group can give some explanation of why they are meeting and what they are doing, and can describe their procedure and purpose. Bion also sees the group as being at the same time in one of three "*basic assumption cultures*" which will be more or less dominant and apparent according to the strength of the work group and the coherence of the group organisation. The existence and continuation of the group, according to Bion's formulation, is threatened by a conflict between what he calls the "group mentality", to which all members contribute, and the individual drives of each group member. The function of the basic assumption cultures is to meet this threat and to ensure the group's continuance. The first of these cultures is dominated by the basic assumption *dependency*, in which the group is seeking some leader, external object, idea, or cause which will dominate it and give it protection and greater cohesiveness. The second basic assumption he calls *fight-flight*, and in this culture the group pinpoints a particular threat which must be dealt with by either fighting it or fleeing from it. The last basic assumption is *pairing* when anxiety compels individual members to seek allies, and this may take place actually, vicariously, or symbolically, and can again be seen as an attempt to increase the cohesiveness of the group. Each basic assumption culture requires a leader, to satisfy dependency, to direct the group in the direction of fight or flight, or to permit pairing. The group is always seeking a leader of a type dictated by the particular basic assumption culture in which it finds itself at any one time. The leader of the basic assumption group is unlikely to be identical with the leader of the work group. At any time, in any group, one of the three basic assumption cultures will be operating alongside the work group. When a basic assumption culture ceases to give sufficient protection, there will be a move into one of the other two cultures. Participation in basic assumption activity is "instantaneous, inevitable, and instinctive", and every group contains a spontaneous cohesive factor based upon mutual basic assumption needs. Bion gives the term "valency" to "the individual's readiness to enter into combination with the group in making and acting on the basic assumptions". Every group is engaged in a struggle, which never ends, to make the work group overcome the basic assumption cultures, and "despite the influence of the basic assumptions, it is the work group that triumphs in the long run". This is compatible with Freud's dictum, "Where id was, ego shall be."

We have referred to the use of psychoanalytic concepts. To be more precise, Bion regards the group activity as a regression to the earliest stages of mental life, and therefore finds his explanations in terms used by Melanie Klein.[1] In his work he gives central importance to projective identification and to the interplay between paranoid-schizoid and depressive positions.

Another framework for studying the behaviour of the group as a whole is supplied by the concepts of Group Analytic Psychotherapy formulated by Foulkes. Foulkes makes use of the concept of a group matrix, a network comprising all the communications and interactions that have taken place in a group from its inception to the present. The matrix, which is equivalent to the history of the group, is growing and develop-ing all the time and becoming more and more complex. "It is the *common shared ground* which ultimately determines the meaning and significance of all events and upon which all communications, verbal and non-verbal, exist". Specific group events take place against the background of this matrix, and cannot be understood in isolation. It is only when they are "located", that is, related to their context of the group matrix, that their significance and meaning can be com-prehended. It is the concept of the group matrix that makes it possible for the group analyst to regard all spontaneous contributions as equivalent to the free association of psycho-analysis. "Looked at this way it becomes easier to understand our claim that the group associates, responds, and reacts as a whole. The group, as it were, avails itself now of one speaker, now of another, but it is always the transpersonal network which is sensitized and gives utterance, or responds. In this

[1] An explanation of the terms used by Melanie Klein may be found in *The Adult World and Other Essays* by Melanie Klein, Heinemann, 1963, and *Introduction to the Theories of Melanie Klein* by Hannah Segal, Heinemann, 1964.

sense we can postulate the existence of a group 'mind' in the same way as we postulate the existence of an individual mind."[1]

The approaches to group work, based on psychoanalytical concepts, assume not only that all the successive events that take place in the group are linked together associatively but also that these events are related to feelings experienced in the current situation. Stock Whitaker and Lieberman, whose focal conflict theory we refer to next, express this with their usual clarity.

"Whatever is said in the group is seen as being elicited not only by the strictly internal concerns of the individual, but by the interpersonal situation in which he finds himself. Of all the personal issues, worries, impulses, and concerns which a patient might express during a group session, what he actually expresses is elicited by the character of the situation. Moreover, a comment is likely to include a number of elements and is responded to selectively by others. An individual may make a comment which includes a half dozen elements. As the others listen to an individual's highly personal contribution, they will respond to certain aspects and ignore others. The aspects which are picked up and built upon are in some way relevant to the other patients and gradually become an emerging shared concern. . . . The group-relevant aspect of an individual's comment is defined by the manner in which the other patients react to it."[2]

This shared aspect of the group, the transpersonal perspective, the behaviour of the group as a whole, is seen by Stock Whitaker and Lieberman in terms of an attempt on the part of the members of the group to establish a generally acceptable solution to a problem, of which they may not be consciously aware, that is affecting them all. This problem is known as the

[1] S. H. Foulkes, *Therapeutic Group Analysis*, Geo. Allen & Unwin Ltd., 1964.

[2] Stock Whitaker and M. A. Lieberman, *Psychotherapy through the Group Process*, Tavistock Publications, 1965, and Atherton Press, New York.

"focal conflict". Such a conflict, representing the covert shared concern of all members, emerges in every group, but the more structured, consistent, and purposeful the group, the harder it will be to detect. It is a conflict between a wish (known in this context as a disturbing motive) and an associated fear (reactive motive), both activated by the current situation in the group. At any time, the behaviour of members of a small group can be seen as determined by the need to find a solution to the current focal conflict. To be successful, the solution must be accepted by them all and must reduce the fears while it permits the maximum possible satisfaction of the wish.

Ezriel has a similar orientation, as is shown in the following:

> "The manifest content of discussion in groups may embrace practically any topic. They might talk about astronomy, philosophy, politics, or even psychology; but it is one of the essential assumptions for psychoanalytic work with groups that, whatever the manifest content may be, there always develops rapidly an underlying common group problem, a common group tension of which the group is not aware, but which determines its behaviour."[1]

In Ezriel's formulation, each member brings into the group an individual unconscious tension, the residue of unresolved infantile conflicts, and he attempts to relieve this tension by means of the relationships which he establishes in the group. To this end, he attempts to manipulate the other members of the group so that they will behave in certain ways which will satisfy his unconscious needs "like pawns in a private game of chess". It is by means of the interaction of each member's individual dominant (unconscious) tension that the "common group tension" is created. Like Stock Whitaker and Lieberman, Ezriel describes the group situation in terms of a dynamic triad of forces. The relationship which the group (or

[1] H. Ezriel, A psychoanalytic approach to group treatment, *British Journal of Medical Psychology*, Vol. XXIII, Parts 1 and 2, 1950.

it could be an individual) is attempting to establish he calls "the required relationship". It is required not so much for the gratification which it is expected to supply, as for its power to prevent an alternative relationship. This alternative he calls "the avoided relationship", for in unconscious phantasy it must be avoided lest it lead to a third situation, "the calamity". For example, a group may behave in a docile and compliant way towards their leader because in this way they create the relationship that is required in order to avoid another type of relationship in which hostility to the leader might find expression and which might bring about the calamity of his withdrawal or retaliation.

Despite their differences, the writers on group psychotherapy we have considered share some important concepts about the nature of groups that are fundamental to their theories. They all recognise the existence of certain processes which are present in every group and which are the overall determinants of the group's behaviour. In psychotherapeutic groups, the processes have a special significance, since, in the words of Stock Whitaker and Lieberman, they "encompass and intersect the individual's concerns in such a way that the individual's therapeutic experience cannot be understood except as it occurs in and through the group processes".

We find ourselves turning from a consideration of the individual to a consideration of the group, and then back again to the individual. This movement between the whole and the parts is important, for both perspectives only have meaning in relation to the other one. The psychological processes that take place within the individual, and within the group of which the individual forms a part, cannot be understood in isolation.

This is the framework within which the experiences of the individual patient must now be considered. Traditionally, group psychotherapy is practised in a medical setting or under medical supervision, and the group member is a "patient", a designation which implies that he is suffering from some condition which requires treatment and which may be cured. There is dissatisfaction with his functioning in one or more areas of his life, and a belief that he could do better. His difficulties may be canalised into a specific symptom or symptoms, but in joining a psychotherapeutic group he is exposing himself to the possibility of a change that will affect not only a specific area of malfunctioning but the whole of his personality, and he is (theoretically at any rate) committing the whole of his personality to the therapeutic process. It is an axiom of all psychotherapy, individual and group, that problems of personality have their origins in early disturbances of interpersonal relationships, that they manifest themselves currently in disturbed interpersonal relationships, and that it is only in interpersonal situations that they can be treated satisfactorily. Individual psychotherapy is an interpersonal situation involving two persons, whereas group psychotherapy involves more than two. Group psychotherapy, it is claimed, provides each group member with experiences which can bring about comprehensive and beneficial personality changes, curing his neurosis, removing his difficulties, and enabling him to relinquish habitual mal-adaptive ways of behaving. The testimony of patients is not enough to substantiate this claim. In addition, the total experience of the individual member in a therapeutic group needs to be examined, and the specific therapeutic components of that experience identified. There seems to be some agreement among writers on Group Psychotherapy about the presence of these components, but opinions differ as to their relative value and importance.

In our model, the psychotherapeutic group is composed of about eight members and a leader. There will be some selection, although the criteria for selection vary from leader to leader and from group to group. In selecting the group, there is likely to be an attempt to avoid great discrepancies in terms of age, intelligence, educational background, and previous experience of therapy. There is also likely to be selection in order to obtain either a one-sex group, or, alternatively, a group in which the sexes are evenly balanced, thus avoiding a situation in which either men or women would constitute a distinct minority. Some forms of illness or personality difficulties may be considered unsuitable for groups altogether, or for one particular group. Stock Whitaker and Lieberman attach importance to selecting a group of patients who are homogeneous in terms of "vulnerability", meaning by vulnerability the extent of the patients' capacity, or lack of capacity, to deal with stressful situations and to tolerate anxiety. There is a danger that if the group is too homogeneous in respect of the habitual methods of dealing with difficulties, the members would then collectively support and reinforce similar habitual mal-adaptive patterns of behaviour.

Our model group meets at least once a week, and remains together for a fixed period of up to an hour and a half. The members sit in a circle. They are expected to communicate freely whatever is in their minds, including their feelings about the group, about other members, and about the leader. There are no limits to the communications. This form of communication has been described as the group equivalent of the "free association" of individual psychoanalysis, in which the patient is expected to reveal all the ideas and associations which come into his mind without regard for their apparent lack of coherence or relevance. Group members cannot communicate in exactly this way, as they each inevitably spend more time in listening than in talking. However, they are encouraged, as far as is possible, to contribute uncensored thoughts and associations, the result being what Foulkes has labelled "free group association". This he treats as the equivalent of the individual's free association although it comes from the group as a whole.

This requires relaxation of the censorship that is normally applied to the expression of thoughts and feelings in social situations. This relaxation is possible only if members of the group come to feel more secure than they would in other settings, and free from the constraints, obligations, and fears that ordinarily prevail. This safety does not mean, of course, that personal criticism or direct verbal attack should be precluded; very much the reverse. It does mean that freedom of expression is seen to belong to them all, that it will be kept by the leader within "safe" bounds, and there will be no repercussions or leaks outside the group.

For this reason, it is important in our model that the members of the group should be strangers to each other, and that any contact between them outside the group meetings be kept to the absolute minimum. Relationships within the group must be kept strictly separated from the personal relationships of domestic and occupational life. These latter are relationships which should not be jeopardised, and the obligations and responsibilities to the continuing life outside the group should not be disregarded.

We must stress that we are describing an idealised model, and for our purposes we are disregarding certain group activities which in other contexts are included within the definition of group psychotherapy by other workers. There are many derivatives of group psychotherapy, for example "therapeutic communities", which have been developed in some hospitals, and in which some of the working activities within the hospital may be intermingled with group meetings. Other types of therapeutic groups include those intended for the treatment of marital disorders, which involve both spouses, and those in which family groups are dealt with as a single unit or together with other families. These need specialised description. For our purpose we are restricting our descriptions to the type of psychotherapeutic group with the properties outlined above.

This psychotherapeutic group has no other structure. No focus is suggested, nor is any topic for discussion supplied. Any external control, however minimal, would deflect the course of the group's free development and interfere with the expression of fundamental conflicts. Members of the group may be told that they are expected to talk, since ultimately group psychotherapy must rely on verbal communication, but even this requirement involves some interference and some distortion. Talking can itself be a defensive activity, used to prevent the development of revealing silences, and to distract attention from important non-verbal communications.

In this unstructured and protected situation, the newcomer to the group is likely to find himself attempting to communicate with the other members about his situation and his personal difficulties. The other group members may, or may not, have been selected on the basis of some shared problem, but in any case they are all people who have acknowledged the existence of difficulties and who are prepared to discuss them with others. This in itself provides him with certain opportunities and experiences. He will realise that he is not the only person who has difficulties, that others have feelings of fear, shame, resentment, and inadequacy, perhaps similar to his own. This is a simple group phenomenon, which has been labelled "universalisation", and which should help to reduce the sense of isolation and shame, and to encourage further communications and even greater frankness.

The responses of others to his communications may help the individual member to see himself in a different light, giving him information about himself and his effect upon other people which has never been available to him before. This is sometimes known as "the Mirror Reaction", perhaps containing an unintended reference to the distorting mirrors of the fairground. The visitor entering one of these "halls of mirrors" is surrounded by reflections of himself, each of which may contain some truth but none of which gives the "true" picture. This type of "feed-back" is something that each gives and each receives, as increasing freedom of expression brings benefits to them all.

"Spectator Therapy" is another term which is sometimes used to indicate the benefits the individual may derive from listening to a discussion of some problem resembling his own, and witnessing attempts to apply different solutions to similar difficulties, even though he may not feel able or willing to contribute to the discussion himself. Any group will include both talkative and less talkative members. Although the importance of verbal communication is rightly stressed, the silent member will also be participating and communicating, at a non-verbal level, even through his silence. Even if he says little, he may be feeling much. None the less, the growth and development of the ability to communicate in words about personal difficulties, to make one's feelings explicit and understood, and to help others to do the same, can indicate the progress of the individual and of the group.

Participation in the group provides the individual member with two different types of information : he hears about the problems of the other members, and he perceives their reactions to his own communications. Each disclosure leads to another, and as the other members put more and more of their cards on the table he finds it increasingly possible to do likewise. Thus the information available to him becomes more relevant and more important. He may be able to test out the possibility of behaving and responding in new ways, and find that there is no need to be so dominant or so self-effacing, so suspicious or so ingratiating, in his personal relationships. Such disadvantageous behaviour may be part of an individual's habitual pattern because he fears the consequences of behaving otherwise. In the special conditions of the group he may feel safe enough to relinquish part of this habitual pattern, only to discover that the feared consequences do not follow. This opportunity for reality-testing that the group provides is stressed by some group psychotherapists, who see it as a necessary forerunner to any therapeutic change.

The individual experiences that we have described so far are likely to be familiar to everyone, and are not the monopoly of psychotherapeutic groups. They may be provided fortuitously in any small face-to-face gathering, particularly where one feels accepted and "at home". A person may find that his life has been changed through a conversation in a railway carriage with a perfect stranger, but the method cannot be taught. Psychotherapeutic groups are different from these casual encounters in that conscious attempts are made to foster these experiences, to maximise their impact, and to call attention to, and study scientifically, what is taking place.

So far we have mentioned the physical setting and the composition of our model group, both designed to promote conditions of greater safety, encourage freer communication, and enable the patient to bring into, or transfer to, the group conflicts and disturbances originally and currently experienced elsewhere.

Though the different theories we have mentioned stress different phenomena and different experiences, all pay some attention to the concept of transference. This concept, central to individual psychoanalytic therapy, needs modification before it can be applied in a group setting. In a two-person setting, the assumption is that the patient transfers to the psycho-therapist feelings experienced in his earliest relationships that are still inappropriately active in his current life. Thus these transferred feelings have two characteristics, their roots in infancy and their current distorting effect on the patient's interpersonal relationships. In most systems of Group Psycho-therapy, it is not considered appropriate to trace transferred emotions back to their historical origins, and emphasis is placed upon their second aspect, the role they play in the "here and now" situation in which all the members of the group are involved.

The transference that takes place in a group differs in several respects from transference in an individual psychotherapeutic setting. Essentially, it has more dimensions. The patient may transfer to the leader, to other members of the group and to the group as a whole. The leader, as a recipient of transference of relationships, aims to remain neutral, and to keep his own personality from intruding. This is not true of the other group members, who will react spontaneously and repudiate any transference roles that do not happen to meet their own needs.

The patient may attempt to re-create in the group the original "network" of relationships in which his conflict was experienced, using different individuals, including the leader, to represent different protagonists. Equally the group itself may come to represent or symbolise something important to the patient. This may be a person, an idea, an object, or a situation. The "matrix" of the group may appropriately stand for the mother. Alternatively, it may represent home, a symbol of security, or an experience like the first day at school.

These are not the only possibilities. Any transference relationship may be shared and divided among different members of the group. In the transference to the leader, which is a feature of all groups, each member may express a different and complementary component. The roles that the members take up in the group may have the same complementarity as the roles assumed within a family, where the good son and the bad son enact their parts in relation to expectations which they share with the parents, and thus the whole network may be transferred into the group with a new dramatis personae.

This is the means by which the patient brings into the group the conflicts and difficulties that he is experiencing elsewhere. The language used to describe the effect of these transferred relationships will vary according to whichever theory is being used. They influence the development of one or other of the basic assumptions; they contribute to the formation of the group matrix; or they help to determine what manner of group focal conflict, or common group tension, develops. The pattern of the communications in the group will be influenced in some way by the theoretical position which the group leader holds.

Up to this point, no specific mention has been made of the role played by the leader, or group psychotherapist. The task of the leader is to influence the development of the group in such a way that each member is able to derive the maximum therapeutic benefit from his attendance at the group sessions. It cannot be taken for granted that group activity (even psychotherapeutic group activity) brings automatic benefit

Groups contain potentialities for harm as well as for good. Fears and anxieties may be confirmed rather than reduced when they are found to be shared by other people; "feed-back" may supply distorted and misleading information; mal-adaptive patterns of behaviour may come to be shared and receive support instead of being challenged. The group may fail to develop and mature; it may encourage regression to earlier levels of development; it may become dependent on its leader, and seduce the leader into playing a directive role. Individual members may be victimised, isolated, attacked, turned into scapegoats, to a degree which they are unable to tolerate. Finally, the group may break up, leaving behind it a residue of disappointment, failure and mistrust.

In the same way that cohesive and disruptive forces co-exist in every group, so the effect of the group on the individual can be ego-strengthening or ego-weakening, therapeutic or anti-therapeutic. Any group will contain both elements. In a psychotherapeutic group, the very factors that support and sustain the individual member support and sustain him in order to expose him to increasing stress and pain. As his endurance increases, so he is given more to endure. As the group gets stronger, so destructive aspects can be more clearly and openly expressed, and the group finds itself able to tolerate such expression, and survive increasingly greater stresses. This cannot be achieved easily. But if the individual patient does not encounter difficult, and unpleasant, and frightening, situations during his group psychotherapy, he will leave the group untouched, his conflicts still intact.

The phenomenon known as "scape-goating", for example, which can occur in all societies and in all groups, can be extremely painful both for the scapegoat and for the other participants. Impulses which a number of members of the group find unacceptable in themselves, and which, if revealed, would cause a breaking-up of the group, may be projected on to one group member. This process allows the remaining members to attack and repudiate such impulses. This way of dealing with what is personally unacceptable may not only secure the continuance of the group, but also it may provide an experience that is necessary for both "scapegoat" and "persecutors", involving and highlighting the basic conflicts of both parties. The two roles are complementary and each contains its own opposite. Group and scapegoat alike find that they can pass through a frightening experience and survive it. On the other hand, either scapegoat or attacker may find the experience intolerable, and may even have to leave the group. Therefore the leader must be able to maintain the delicate balance. One side of the balance is to allow sufficient stressful interaction to represent the inevitable conflictful situations that have to be experienced, and which all recur in everyday life. The other side is to prevent the stress on any individual from extending to a breakdown that would damage victim and victimisers alike.

In an earlier chapter we put forward the concept that group processes are determined by the struggle between cohesive and disruptive elements in the group, and, by the same token, in the individuals composing the group. The existence of the group is constantly threatened by the disruptive forces in the group and in the individual members, and measures have to be taken by the group as a whole to meet this threat and safeguard its continuance. Scapegoating can be one such measure. This concept seems to be present, if not always explicitly stated, in most dynamic group theories.

A close analogy may be drawn between the group and the nation state. The disruptive elements in the state can be dealt with in a variety of ways. A strong state may be able to tolerate rebellious and even subversive activity on the part of minority groups such as students and others, whereas a weak and divided state is more likely to curtail freedom of speech and assembly, introduce censorship, and attempt to secure conformity to its rulings. In a similar way, some groups may develop a "culture" which discourages non-conformity, puts a virtual taboo on the discussion of certain topics, or makes it only possible to discuss them in certain approved ways. Even the theories believed to be held by the group leader may become an ideology which must not (or must) be challenged.

The term "culture" is used in this way by Stock Whitaker and Lieberman to include "the practices, standards, and mutual understandings which regulate relationships within the group and define the character of the group world". It is the culture which determines what is acceptable and what is not acceptable, and where the limits of tolerance and acceptance lie. In their focal conflict theory, Stock Whitaker and Lieberman see the culture as being made up of the sum of all the successful solutions to the focal conflicts that have been preoccupying the group at an unconscious or near-conscious level. These solutions are described as either restrictive or enabling. A restrictive solution to a group focal conflict is like repressive state action, the group as a whole deciding to deal with subversive elements by a restriction of freedom.

Although the leader is also subject to the influence of the group culture, he must be able to maintain sufficient detachment from it so that he is aware of what is going on and can intervene to influence it. He must be able to recognise the group processes, and the way in which each individual member is contributing to them and being influenced by them. He must be able to recognise his own involvement in the group processes and forecast how the others will be influenced by any intervention, or lack of intervention, on his part.

We can distinguish a number of different ways in which the group psychotherapist influences the group. Every intervention that he makes, or does not make, will have its significance. First of all, there is his implicit attitude. His behaviour will to some extent serve as a model for the members of the group. It is through his attitude, rather than anything that he says, that he shows the group the importance of tolerance, and promotes a permissive and accepting atmosphere. He has to help the group to tolerate distressing experiences by his own ability to tolerate them. Initially, and in the last resort, he guarantees the safety of the group, and the members need to feel that he is capable of doing this, and that, whatever they do or say, he will not be frightened or angry, wounded or destroyed. His tranquillity provides some protection against the disruptive forces, the fears, and conflicts, and antagonisms, which might destroy the group. If *he* can withstand the contents, Pandora may open her box.

He is used as a transference figure by the group, and he must accept this, even if he does not deliberately encourage it. He wishes to help all the group members to become as fully involved as possible, to relate not only to him but also to each other, and to look to each other for reactions to, and comments on, their communications. He does not wish to be the main focus in the group, neither does he wish to "lead" it. It is for this reason that Foulkes does not use the term "leader" but prefers to speak of a group "conductor". The leader is not a leader and neither is he a teacher nor yet a counsellor. The group may try to cast him in one of these roles and he will need to consider this attempt, as he will all other group happenings, in relation to the state of the group as a whole and the processes operating in it. He will perhaps consider that the attempt means that the group as a whole is trying to avoid dealing with some particular problem, is showing a reluctance to take the next step forward, is wishing instead to substitute some magical solution and to return to a state of dependence upon a parental figure. The progress of every psychotherapeutic group is hindered by obstacles. These obstacles are introduced by individual members and accepted by the group as a whole because they afford a temporary solution to, or respite from, a current group problem, or because they prevent change in an unknown and therefore frightening direction. Everything that the leader does, or does not do, in this situation will affect the outcome. He needs to be aware of the group processes, of the way in which each individual is contributing to the group processes, and of their relevance to, and effect upon, each individual. Through his tacit refusal to accept the role pressed upon him, by denying the group a magical solution or a dependent relationship, he may be able to re-confront it with the problem which it is trying to evade. Or he may judge it necessary to put into words what is going on and to draw the attention of the group to the meaning of its own behaviour. This brings us to the unique aspect of the psychotherapist's role in the group, his analytic function of "making the unconscious conscious" through his interpretations.

The interpretations of the leader in our group therapy model differ from those of the individual psychotherapist in that they are not centred upon individuals and, therefore, they do not attempt to trace the transference relationship back to its historical roots. For the past history of each individual is separate and unique and belongs to that individual alone; it is only in the "here and now" situation in the group that individual concerns meet, and that a focus can be found which belongs to all members conjointly and which conjointly affects them all. Each member is a co-author of the theme. Even if the leader does not presume to believe in something as mystical as a "group unconscious", he behaves as if every communication can, in some sense, be taken to come from the group as a whole. This means that his assignment is to find the factor in the communication that has reference to a common preoccupation of the group. References to individuals are not necessarily precluded. The leader may need to make an interpretation about the behaviour of a particular group member, where the interests of the group and of the individual require it, but every such decision will be made with reference to the processes operating in the group at that time. It will also need to be made in the awareness that the singling out of an individual by the leader can be destructive to both individual and group, and is not to be undertaken without good cause.

An interpretation has to be well timed. If given prematurely, it may seem like an attack, increasing the threat to the group and the need for a defensive solution; or it may bring a potentially valuable experience to an untimely end. It could also forestall the finding of the interpretation by the group as a whole, and the group would be so much the poorer. Each member in the group has a role as therapist, as well as patient, and needs to exercise that role. Rather than presenting the group members with his interpretations (and thereby emphasising dependence upon him), the leader may help them to find their own, asking questions rather than suggesting answers. For there is no role, whether that of guarantor of safety, protector of the weak, interpreter, clarifier, or therapist, that the leader would not rather see exercised by the group working together than arrogate to himself.

The advantages that group therapy can bring to the individual are equalled by the potential dangers, which are greater than in either of our other two systems. Analytical therapy demands commitment, a greater commitment than in any other structured encounter. No one ever commits the whole of himself to this process, not even in individual analysis. Yet, in analysis, whether individual or group, it is not possible to anticipate nor to define the areas of confrontation, nor to contract out of any one of them in advance. *It is the potentiality of commitment which is without limits.* This potentiality makes group therapy a more dangerous situation for patient and therapist than exists in Group Counselling or in Group Discussion, where group members may legitimately make mental reservations which keep some part of themselves untouched. The danger in Group Psychotherapy lies in the unwitting exposure of vulnerable parts of the personality, the removal of defences, and the release of forces which could well be destructive in and to the personalities of the partici-pants. These are the forces which are the springs of all creative activity; but the same forces, unharnessed and undirected, are the essence of psychosis and violence.

The development of the group's capacity to deal with its

destructive forces must not be weakened or impaired, since in participation of this development we find a large part of the individual's therapeutic experience. However, the expression of destructive forces may at times outstrip the capacity of the group to tolerate them without damage, and the vulnerability of different group members will vary. In the language of psychiatric practice we are accustomed to use the phrase "acting out" to describe behaviour which is undesirable or even disastrous, whereas a description of phantasies of the same behaviour would be welcomed as a revelation of unconscious processes. Some of the activities and exchanges within the process of Group Psychotherapy might well be called "acting out". For example, members of the group may make sexual challenges to each other. These might well represent the recognition of sexual feelings in their manifold form. There is a legitimate place for the expression of these feelings, which exist in human encounters in a variety of forms and which ordinarily must remain unrecognised and unexpressed. However, in Group Psychotherapy, someone must take the responsibility for preventing these expressions from becoming dangerous seductions or attacks. The absence of limits for discussion is not the absence of limits for action.

The leader has a duty which is similar to that of the individual psychotherapist. Necessary as it is for the deepest unconscious material to be revealed, the psychotherapist must at some point relate it back to conscious material. Insight is not the equivalent of the revelation of unconscious material alone; it is the perception of both conscious and unconscious meanings at the same time. Similarly, in Group Psychotherapy, the group psychotherapist may have to remind the participants of the existence of the outside world.

We have referred to the skills which the psychotherapist needs to have. These skills include the ability to reintroduce limits in a situation where the limits have been removed. This is not merely the ability to restrict something which he fears or does not understand. He has to be able to perceive the trends and to be able to carry himself along into the same depths as the participants. He has to have the ability and the experience to keep part of himself as an observer of the conscious as well as the unconscious meanings, and to predict the way in which the discussion will affect the feelings and behaviour of all the group members. He has to be able to intervene and, equally important, he has to be able to remain silent.

Finally, we can only agree with Foulkes that the responsibility is great and that "no one should embark on this who has not the measure and control of his power firmly in his blood and system, lest he will suffer the fate of the sorcerer's apprentice".

It was intended to be part of our purpose to describe Group Psychotherapy as a separate process, in terms that would distinguish it clearly and unambiguously from Group Counselling and Group Discussion. We believe that we have been able to draw some valid distinctions. We have, however, to admit that in a very real sense Group Psychotherapy can only be identified as those procedures that are carried out by individuals with the following qualifications : they are psycho-analysts or psychotherapists who have had an additional training in group methods, who therefore have authorisation to treat patients by this means. We acknowledge that this definition is comparable to the definition of psychiatric illness as that illness which is treated by a psychiatrist. Group Psychotherapy is that which is practised by group psychotherapists.

CHAPTER 6

Group Counselling

IN DISCUSSING group work so far, enough has been said to make it clear that we are not using the term Group Counselling to describe a form of Group Psychotherapy that has been diluted in order to allow it to be carried out by less-skilled practitioners. It is used, rather, to denote a distinct process in which a different form of help is offered, with aims, criteria, techniques, and skills of its own. It draws upon dynamic theories of group behaviour derived from Group Psychotherapy, but it makes use of them to serve its own different purpose. It also draws upon theories of social casework, but this does not make it a technique to be used exclusively by social workers. It is not confined within the boundaries of any one profession. However, social workers are likely to remain its principal and most steadfast practitioners; it is in social work settings that its concepts can be most clearly demonstrated. It is, therefore, in relation to social work that we shall mainly be considering it.

In contrasting Group Counselling and Group Psychotherapy, one essential distinction has already been made. In Group Counselling, as in casework, a particular aim is detected and defined at the outset, providing a focus and setting the limits within which the proceedings of the group take place. Group Psychotherapy is not so bound. We stress this distinction because, in our opinion, group work that is not defined and limited requires the sanctions of psychotherapy, and only someone possessing the skills of a group psychotherapist is authorised

to practise it. Outside this discipline, unstructured and unfocused work is hazardous for both leader and members of
the group.

Thus so far, in attempting to establish a second group
system, the emphasis has been placed upon the more restricted
purpose of Group Counselling, the lack of sanction for the
type of free disclosure required by psychotherapy, and the
less complete commitment of the participants.

The limitation in aims means that Group Counselling is
less intensive and less comprehensive, but, by the same token,
it is more flexible and has a wider application, extending to
situations where the rigorous demands of Group Psychotherapy
would not be met. Members of a counselling group come for a
limited purpose; they are not required to be patients, accepting
a status that has implications of weakness and dependency,
and neither do they need to be strangers to each other nor
to restrict their contacts outside the group meetings. Group
Counselling need not be confined to the consulting room but
can be practised in a variety of different settings, and it can
be used to deal with groups that are already in existence as
well as the artificial groups created specifically for a treatment
purpose, though here care may have to be taken to find an
appropriate point of focus. Group counsellors may belong to
a number of different disciplines: given a professional competence in one particular area, such as medicine, nursing,
psychology, or teaching, individual helping methods can be
augmented and extended by the acquisition of group counselling techniques.

To say that Group Counselling does not deal with the
deeper levels of personality is not to say that it is less valuable.
It is necessary to emphasise this point because the great
influence and prestige of analytic practice has sometimes
suggested that any other method is second best. In the past,
social workers themselves have helped to establish this hierarchy
of esteem by valuing more highly those forms of casework that
make most use of interpretation and the development of

insight. Attempts are now being made to reverse this trend. Treatment in "depth" no longer seems to be the preferred technique in all circumstances. It is now increasingly recognised that different levels of work are appropriate in different circumstances, and the optimum level may be that which achieves sufficient result with the minimum of disturbance. By analogy, you do not need deep mining to obtain open-cast coal, and, for that matter, in some countries diamonds can be picked up on the surface. The only justification for going "deep"[1] is that in some situations it is necessary to do so.

Depth is one dimension. It is not the only one. We need to look at this dimension along with others, and so we need to consider a number of different approaches, involving a number of different professions, to the assessment and treatment of personal problems. This requires a concept of a total treatment process as a context in which different dimensions, levels, or areas of work can be related as alternatives or complements to each other. This context must be able to include different forms of analytic and psychological treatment, social work, Group Counselling, and Group Psychotherapy.

Before adding our own formulation to the many that have gone before, a word or two of qualification is needed. No formulation such as that of a total treatment process can ever be definitive or complete. More than that, it can lead to self-deception, obscuring rather than clarifying the processes that are actually taking place. In describing what we are doing we

[1] We have used the word "deep", in good company, in a rather vague way. "Deep" can mean going a long way back into personal history, and behind the memories that are first paraded. Alternatively, it can mean an exploration of aspects of mental functioning that are normally hidden by dynamic repressive forces. The word "deep" is used metaphorically, and there are fallacies in any such concept. For example, the content of this "deep" level has features in common with psychotic thinking, and similar material may in fact be that which is first offered by psychotic patients.

risk becoming the dupes of our own propaganda and our own legends, and it is often the incomplete formulations of the past that have provided our current myths by which we are bemused. The myth that is currently fashionable, for example, is that we deal with the total person in his total environment. This is indeed the general aim. The aim is unattainable, though there may be increased satisfaction, and an improvement in methods, every time that the area which is dealt with is enlarged. The concept of the total person in his total environment is an abstraction; its purpose is to remind us of the unattainable aim, and to indicate such extensions in understanding as have been achieved.

When we attempt to study the total patient, or client, all that we are able to comprehend and describe are a few fragments of an unknown whole. When the patient or client tells us of his problem, he is offering us one fragment. We may respond to that fragment, or we may add to it other fragments which we have comprehended through our own observations or from other sources. The field to which these fragments belong is complex and unbounded; in order to do our work we have to simplify it and to put in some boundaries, and our concepts and formulations are our attempts to do this.

In our formulation of the total treatment process, we suggest that the fragments which are obtained can be classified under three main headings, representing three areas of the patient's total functioning. Any single process that is undertaken in the way of treatment must be directed to one of these three areas. They are as follows:

1. *The patient's circumstances,* including his material environment, his education or work, and his financial and housing situation.
2. *The patient's personality,* including his state of physical and mental health, his defects and disorders, his capacities and potentialities.

3. *The network of interpersonal relationships* of which the patient forms a part, including his family of origin and his current parental, marital, and social relationships.

Any problem may be presented by the patient or by others as a malfunctioning in any one, or more than one, of these three areas. The area chosen will often determine which of the caring professions is given authority to intervene. A professional helper, though he should not ignore the expressed area, may consider another one to be equally, or more, significant. These areas are not alternatives: they exist simultaneously and they are interconnected. If intervention takes place in one area, the others will not remain unaffected. In our view, no one area can be satisfactorily treated in isolation. Neither is any one discipline professionally equipped on its own to intervene directly in all three. Where social workers attempt to deal with two areas simultaneously, they are likely to look on one area as the primary one, and the attribution of primary and secondary importance to one or another factor may depend upon the credo of the worker. There are, indeed, professional people who, as an ideological principle, restrict all their efforts to one of these areas and question the relevance of any of the others. Some psychiatrists, for example, will hold that all that is necessary is to deal with a disorder within the individual personality; they treat the disease, restore the patient to his previous good health, and the patient himself then deals with the external circumstances and finds that his personal and family relationships have improved! Others may concentrate on social and family relationships, often finding the pathology there, if not the cure. Other workers again have economic and political explanations for all disorder and consequently find it intractable until such time as these external conditions receive their rightful attention in the society in which we live. Alternatively, there are others who take a more global approach, and feel competent to deal with all three areas, by themselves and at the same time. This at least avoids that fragmentation of problems which is now generally deplored, but those who work in this way need to recognise that in much of what they are doing they are making use of their own personal resources and their experience of life rather than their professional training. The general practitioner, for example, who tries himself to deal with the problem as a whole may find that he is having to be an untrained psychotherapist and untrained social worker as well as a trained family doctor.

This formulation of the treatment process can be illustrated in a simple example. A young man has difficulty in finding and keeping a job. The work that he is equipped to do is in short supply in his neighbourhood. He has specific neurotic difficulties which affect his application to his work. These difficulties are fostered by his dependent relationship with the mother with whom he lives. In this example, the problem could be located in any or all of the three areas, and the initial intervention might be directed at any one of them or at more than one. But intervention in each area involves a distinct and different process. Treatment directed at his circumstances, such as the finding of jobs for him, retraining him for a different job, or intervening with his employers, is a process which has no direct group counterpart, and so, although important, it does not directly concern us here. Treatment directed at the area of his personality may be offered on an individual basis or as a group process; as a group process it has been considered in the previous chapter on Group Psychotherapy. We are left with the third area, and, correspondingly, with a third treatment process. In this, the focus is not upon the intra-personal conflicts of the patient but upon his interpersonal relationships, and therefore it takes in not only the patient but also the whole network of relationships of which he forms a part. Treatment will consist of intervention at any point in this network; it may involve work directly with the referred patient, or it may involve work with some other key person such as parent or spouse. We have mentioned

hypothetical case above in which a young man's difficulties
were intensified by his relationship with his mother, and
therefore, in this instance, the relationship between mother
and son might be selected as the focus of a treatment process.
Treatment focused upon this relationship might involve work
directly with the young man himself : such work would have a
limited aim and would fall within the framework which
belongs to casework rather than to psychotherapy. On the
other hand, treatment might take the form of interviews with
the mother in the interests of her son. This would involve
working with someone who does not see herself in the role
of a patient, and within a different set of sanctions. She
may, however, have access to sufficient anxiety about her
role as a mother to allow her to question it, and to accept
the status of client, in her own right, in relation to a caseworker.

This area of work is of interest and concern to different
disciplines. Many psychotherapists seek to include it within
their own field. However, where treatment is based upon team
work with a high degree of professional differentiation, it is
usually seen as a specialist province of the social worker. Thus
we have another dimension added to our conception of social
casework; it is within the area of interpersonal relationships
that it finds a major focus and a primary technique. Other
techniques and other forms of help—material, educational, or
psychological—are not excluded, but such help can only be
considered as casework when it is offered within the context
of a personal relationship of a particular kind, and when it
is offered in such a way that it contributes to the development
of that relationship.

What special techniques, then, differentiate work in this
area? We have already considered some of the assumptions
that are made about the nature of interpersonal relationships.
Each one of us lives within a network of interconnected
relationships, and through them we seek to satisfy our basic
emotional needs. It is the whole that gives the parts a special

significance, and it is only in the context of the whole that specific events can be understood. A new and happier situation at work may help a man to make a more positive contribution in his family circle. Conversely, a frustrated wife is more likely to be a possessive mother and an exacting friend. Our relationships with other people are not only interconnected horizontally in the present: they are also connected longitudinally throughout our life history. The interaction that took place between ourselves and others in the past, particularly in our earliest, most formative, years, influences our present needs, and our demands and expectations of others. The extent of the influence varies, as some people are able to achieve a greater freedom from past conflicts than others can, but some influence always remains.

In his professional role, the social worker enters the network of significant relationships surrounding the client and becomes part of it. The relationship that he establishes becomes part of his client's experience and contributes to the whole, affecting not only the client but also all members of the client's immediate circle, and others with whom he comes in contact. It is in the use of this relationship that a large part of the social worker's own particular and distinctive professional skill is shown.

As an illustration of both social work and Group Counselling, we propose to consider work with mothers in a child guidance clinic. Though such a setting cannot be regarded as typical, it is one with which both the authors are familiar, and in which group work belonging to all three of our systems may take place. Here the different areas of work, and the roles of different professions, can be clearly seen. When a child requires treatment, his place in the network of family and school has to be considered. For this reason Child Guidance has always attempted to deal simultaneously with several dimensions and has had a multidisciplinary approach.

The social worker in a child guidance clinic is traditionally expected to contribute to the treatment of the child through

he family interaction. Let us suppose that she[1] chooses to do
his by means of a series of interviews with the child's mother.
t is likely that she will keep the following points in mind. Her
lient is a woman who is meeting difficulties in her role as a
nother, and who has enough awareness of these difficulties to
ccept treatment for herself, albeit on behalf of her child. The
ocial worker is a helping and caring person, in a position of
uthority. The mother–child relationship is therefore to some
xtent mirrored in the relationship with her client. Attitudes
hat have been carried over from the client's earliest relation-
hip with her own mother are likely to be brought into this
elationship. These attitudes are likely to be relevant to the
roblems on which treatment is focused, since it was from this
elationship that the client derived her own primary experience
f mothering.

In addition, every theme of family life has its resonance in
he mother's conception of herself as a mother. Her past
ecollection of being mothered by her parents, aunts, uncles,
nd older siblings are accompanied by present feelings about
er role as supplementary mother to other members of her
xtended family; and there is also the counterpart of this in
er continuing need to be mothered herself by these relatives
nd even by the children. All this is ever present in the mother's
elationship with the child who is the referred patient, and
lso in the mother's relationship with the social worker. The
ocial worker needs to be aware of the range and extent of
ll these feelings and the part that they play in these two
gnificant sets of relationships: the relationship between
other and child on which her work is focused, and her
wn relationship with her client which is her principal
herapeutic tool.

In this professional relationship between social worker and
ient, the social worker will seek to create a situation of safety

[1] Here we have arbitrarily changed the pronoun for the social
orker to the feminine, following the customary practice in
riting on Child Guidance.

in which the client will feel free to discuss her difficulties and her feelings about them without fear of being criticised or misunderstood. The social worker will try to use the relationship sensitively and flexibly to meet what she conceives to be the needs of her client as a person and a mother. She may use the relationship to augment the client's experience, perhaps to make good some deficiency in the past or present that is adversely affecting her maternal role. She may use it to provide a counterbalance to recollections of faulty experiences in the past that the present situation has re-activated. Whatever she does, she exists as a model with which the client may identify providing a pattern of behaviour which can be incorporated and applied in other contexts. Within the particular focus of child guidance, the way in which the social worker behaves towards her client may be taken to exemplify "good" parental behaviour. Ferrard and Hunnybun, in *The Caseworker's Use of Relationships*, discuss the help that can be given to immature people "by slowly building up a relationship with them that offers warmth and understanding, thus enabling them gradually to take over from the worker, as they might from a wise and kindly parent, ideas and ways of behaviour never learnt in childhood."[1]

Within this relationship, the social worker may employ other techniques. She may seek to promote the development of insight and understanding about the problem at a more conscious level. She may use some interpretations. She may encourage the ventilation of hostile feelings, which, once safely expressed and accepted in a casework situation, could lose some of their hurt so that they no longer needed to be directed inappropriately elsewhere. She may also try to educate her client about the norms of child development and about different ways in which difficulties with children could be handled. In all this, the skilled use of the worker–client relationship remains an essential prerequisite and is the context

[1] Margaret L. Ferrard and Noel K. Hunnybun, *The Caseworker's Use of Relationships*, Tavistock Publications, 1962.

within which all other techniques operate. It is only when these other techniques are employed in this context that they become part of casework rather than of some other process.

Although present behaviour is affected by all that has happened in the past, the effect is not static or inevitable. Any fresh experience in the present can give a new significance to past events and modify their current influence. Thus help can be provided by means of such experiences, without the need to work at "deeper" levels and to uncover the events and emotions of the past.

Mothers attending a child guidance clinic may have individual interviews with a social worker, or they may join with other mothers and a social worker in a group. In either case the purpose is the same. The focus is still upon the mother–child relationship and the aim is still a development of this relationship in the interests of the referred child. But the instrument to bring this about is no longer an individual relationship and an individual casework process. It has become a group relationship and a group process, making use of free discussion with others in a like situation and the interaction that takes place among the members and the group counsellor.

Attempts may be made to justify such group work as a time-saver, in that one worker sees a number of mothers at one interview. The process may or may not save time, but some groups may well go more quickly and more intensively into the important areas of discussion simply because the situation itself provides a living experience of some of the issues which in individual casework can only be indirectly described. In the group, the mother finds herself in a situation that is more complex and more diffuse than individual casework. Instead of a two-person relationship designed solely to help her, which can be tailored to meet her own particular requirements, she is placed in a group of her peers and is exposed to the demands of competing needs. It is a situation which is closer to real life, to which current problems and preoccupations may be quickly transferred, and in which feelings are more immediately aroused. The relationship with the group leader is a more diluted one, and some of its aspects are spread out over the other members, but its totality is not necessarily less intense.

We emphasise the difference between Group Counselling and Group Psychotherapy, but it will be seen that Group Counselling offers many of the same advantages and opportunities that have already been discussed in relation to Group Psychotherapy. These advantages and opportunities are no less relevant because the group is bounded by a problem that is known to be shared by all the participants. The group counsellor may work within different terms of reference and different sanctions from a group psychotherapist, and the techniques and skills that she employs may differ in many respects, but both make use of forces that are found in all groups. Whether the group work is limited and problem focused, or whether it is intensive and analytic, engaging the total personalities of the participants, the positive therapeutic factors that exist in the group situation will need to be utilised. Likewise these factors will have their negative, anti-therapeutic, counterparts, and these cannot be ignored.

The mother taking part in a counselling group is not the sole recipient : a position sustaining and gratifying to some, humiliating and threatening to others. In the group she is a giver as well as a receiver; she contributes to its success and to its failure, and to the help that the others receive. She listens and reacts to the problems of others, and her own difficulties are not divulged to one helper under conditions of strict confidentiality, but are exposed to the reactions and comments of a wider circle. If, in an individual interview, she were to disclose emotionally charged information about herself, the response would be carefully handled by the audience of one. In a group, her contribution will be received by the other members, and responded to in the light of their different emotional involvements. Any response made by the group counsellor will have to be geared to the needs of the group as a whole, and not solely to the needs of one particular member.

Every contribution adds something to the group and may be of help to others. Each mother brings to the discussion her own experiences as a mother in relation to her children, and these experiences, in which she may feel she has failed, are used to enrich the proceedings of the group and may be treated as a valuable contribution. Thus through her very failure she is given an opportunity to experience the satisfactions and reassurance of being able to help others. This is an example of the support which a group can supply to its members, which extends beyond anything which could be provided in an individual casework situation. Each mother does not depend upon the individual reassurance provided by a social worker, which, if given, would be likely to increase dependency and allay anxieties in an unproductive way. Instead, she creates her own reassurance from her growing ability to contribute to the group, from the use that is made of her contributions, and from the further contributions of others.

The members of such a group come not as patients but as mothers, and the staff of a child guidance clinic emphasise this by using the term "mothers' group". While discussing the difficulties of this role that they share, there are opportunities to build up confidence in the person behind the role. It may even be possible, in this context, to attack the activities within the role without damaging the person responsible for the activities.

In one group of mothers, one member referred to the fact that her own elderly mother of eighty was ill. She described her anxieties about losing her mother, but accompanied the description with a brilliant smile which seemed intended to reassure herself and to tell the other members that all her feelings were within her control. Another member questioned her as to whether she would be relieved of the burden when her mother died, and gradually in response to further questioning she was induced to admit some of her long-standing hostile feelings about her mother. At this point the group counsellor (in this instance a man and a psychiatrist) was about to draw the session to a close when another member said, "Are we going to allow Mrs. X to go away thinking that she is bad? Oughtn't we to recognise the fact that she is genuinely concerned about her mother?"

If this point had been brought in too early, or if it had been introduced by the person who had made the attack, it would have been no more than the reassuring smile which the mother had used herself. It derived its value from all that had gone before. This reparative part of the work might well have been carried out by the leader, if he had thought of it, but it was far better coming from a member of the group. Indeed, if it had occurred to the leader to make such a contribution, he might on second thoughts have decided to withhold it. Opportunities need to be given to all members of the group to exercise the functions that would, in a one-to-one interview, belong to the professional worker: functions such as acceptance, tolerance, support, and acknowledgement of both aspects of ambivalence. Thus Phillida Parsloe, in "Some thoughts on social group work,[1] writes that the social group worker "has to find ways of working which allow full scope for the members' ability to help each other. This can be difficult for caseworkers, for we have been used in the one-to-one interview to having all to ourselves the powerful and satisfying position of accepting, enabling, and helping. . . . In a group one hopes such support will come from a member, and this may mean the leader has to control not only words but smiles, nods, and hand movements as well, and thus allow space for members to move in to show their acceptance."

The loss of uniqueness, the knowledge of shared difficulties, should do something to reduce the feelings of isolation and shame which cultural attitudes in our society help to induce, and by which problems are often exacerbated. We have already discussed how one confidence often leads to another, and how we find ourselves becoming franker about our own problems in response to a friend's disclosures. After this,

[1] P. Parsloe, Some thoughts on social group work, *British Journal of Psychiatric Social Work*, Vol. X, No. 1, 1969.

problems often appear less intractable and solutions more attainable. In a social setting, the sequel to frank disclosures may be embarrassment and withdrawal at the next encounter. This may also happen in a counselling group. The group counsellor will have to anticipate this possibility, and perhaps even discourage premature exchange of confidences in the beginning stages of a group. A group psychotherapist, on the other hand, is able to permit greater tensions to develop from the very beginning, and the group then has more time to develop its own means for dealing with such problems.

Each member will not only talk about her own difficulties, but will also listen to the difficulties of others, and their descriptions of attempts to cope with problems like and unlike her own. She may become interested in a problem raised by another member and take part in discussing it, without revealing, perhaps without acknowledging even to herself, that it is in fact a resemblance to some part of her own situation that has aroused her interest. Thus she is working indirectly and vicariously on her own difficulties.

Each member in the mothers' group hears of a wider range of attitudes and reactions to common difficulties in family relationships than her own experience could provide. She learns that there are many different ways in which children can be handled. Through identification, she is able to experiment in phantasy, to try on and adopt, or sometimes reject, different modes of behaviour. She thereby is able to extend the range of her own possible responses and repertoires.

Participation in the group may help some mothers to relinquish defences which are preventing them from dealing realistically with their situation. For example, a mother may be unable to give her handicapped child the help he needs because she is preoccupied with attributing blame to medical or educational authorities. It might take a social worker, who is offering individual interviews, a long time to work through this, as any direct approach to this issue would be seen as one authority defending another, and would be likely to reinforce the mother's attitude. Comments from other parents with similar problems would be very differently received. From an early age, we tend to be more easily influenced, favourably or unfavourably, by the opinion of our peer group than by any other.

The comments of other members in this example are less likely to be helpful if some of them have a like attitude towards people in authority. A group composed of people who all make use of similar habitual ways of dealing with their problems may supply support and confirmation for maladaptive patterns of behaviour in which they all have a share. Though this can happen in all our three systems, it is more likely to happen in groups which are focused upon a common problem. (The record of a counselling group given on pages 98–100 below provides an illustration.) The danger lies in such behaviour becoming entrenched as part of the group "culture", as may happen when the behaviour offers a solution not only to individual problems but also to the threat of disruptive forces in the group. If the members can unite in attributing blame elsewhere, they are reducing their own feelings of guilt, finding an outlet for action even if it is of a negative kind, and binding the group together against a common "enemy". This possibility should be borne in mind whenever it is possible to exercise some selection procedure for counselling groups. Such groups are likely to make more rapid progress if there is some diversity in the solutions that members habitually employ to meet their common problems.

The capacity of the members of the group to identify with one another, to discover the common aspects in each individual problem, and to give as well as to receive help, forms an important part of the group counselling process in child guidance as in other settings. It is something that the group counsellor may need to promote, intervening more directly to this end than a group psychotherapist would be likely to do. It is therefore important that the group counsellor should be able to identify correctly the cohesive factors that are present in the group, the areas which can be shared, and the conditions under which sharing is possible: otherwise she may find herself encouraging a spurious uniformity and delaying the discussion of real and important differences. She must also recognise and not be dismayed by the disruptive forces in the group, and these may have to be dealt with if they are relevant to the problem on which the group is focused, or if they are seriously hampering the group's progress. However, she will not seek to bring these negative forces to the fore in the way that might be appropriate in some stages of Group Psychotherapy.

This skill, the capacity to recognise, and make use of, such therapeutic forces as are immediately available, can be studied and acquired; it can also sometimes be recognised in an unlearned, intuitive response. A few years ago there was a meeting of parents and staff at a junior training centre which one of us attended. It was a big meeting with about a hundred parents present, and after the speeches the centre head, who was in the chair, invited questions from the floor.

"Please, Miss," came from the back of the hall, "when will my Jenny be able to walk?"

The centre head appealed to the audience, "Some of you know a lot about this. Come along, you other parents with Mongol children, tell us when your children started to walk."

The meeting at once became lively, with a number of parents eagerly recounting their experiences and an audience listening intently. A large unwieldy meeting had become for the moment an effective group. What the head had done was to make a relationship between the experiences of one member and the experiences of others : a relationship which could then grow and develop.

The context in which group counselling processes take place, and the counterpart of the two-person relationship between client and caseworker, is the relationship between the client and the group as a whole, including the group leader. Just as some mothers benefit from an individual relationship with a caseworker of a kind they have never experienced before, so those who receive group counselling may benefit from a new experience in a relationship with a group. In the group situation different needs will be activated, and a different, perhaps wider, range of feelings will be experienced. Individual casework would be more likely to reveal and deal with particular personal relationships, starting with those with the parents, whereas the relationships transferred to a counselling group will include those with siblings, classmates, and colleagues. Thus the first difficulties to become apparent may be those concerned with rivalry, competing, and sharing, rather than with dependency. The mother who, as a child at school, had to demand attention from the teacher which she did not always receive, and had difficulties in making friends with her fellow pupils, may start with similar problems as a member of a group of mothers. The very act of joining the group has some factors reminiscent of entry into school during infancy, when the child has to abandon her position of exclusive relationship to her own mother and begin one that is shared with other pupils. This new relationship depends for its character on expectations regarding the teacher as well as on the realities of her character and behaviour. These difficulties may form one aspect of the mother's nuclear problem, but they are not the aspect that she would bring first into the individual relationship with a caseworker. The group counsellor needs to be aware of each mother's nuclear problem in all these aspects, and also of the ways in which the aspects are interrelated. In this particular instance, her responsibility to the mother is to try to ensure that what the mother experiences is not merely another sterile repetition of the past relationship as pupil to teacher or amongst peers.

We have emphasised the specific foci of counselling groups, and the maintenance of the specific focus in each group is another responsibility of the group counsellor. In the mothers' group, the group counsellor must herself keep the mothers' problems with their children constantly in mind, and she must also maintain a connection between these problems and all the activities at different levels that are taking place in the group. This should not mean an unnecessary curtailment of freedom of expression, nor should it mean the introduction of artificial, or unhelpful, or untimely, comparisons. The discussion will inevitably range over other topics. For example, the mothers may turn from discussing their children to discussing their husbands, and confidences about their marital situations may be exchanged. The group leader will have to respond to this apparent change of theme. There is a danger that the group may lose contact with its original purpose, becoming an unfocused group or even slipping into a form of group psychotherapy which has not been sanctioned. There is the further danger of entering into the enjoyment of the "pastime", which Berne in his book *Games People Play* described as "Lady talk" with such topics as "Delinquent husbands". This topic can be developed further into one entitled "Aren't husbands awful?", or even "Aren't all men just children?" The group counsellor would not deal with these themes in terms of the individual personality of the woman and her absent husband, as in individual psychotherapy; neither would they be interpreted as an illustration of the narrator's unconscious or undisclosed feelings in relation to other members of the group or to the group as a whole, as might happen in Group Psychotherapy. Rather would they be dealt with as exemplifying the complex interaction between people. They would be placed in a context which includes relationships between parents and parents, parents and children, children and children, either separately or together. The leader is again making links between one relationship and another, and she sees them both as part of an interconnected network with which she is concerned.

As well as the behaviour of individuals in the group, the group counsellor must be aware of what is taking place at a group level, and she will look on the choice of this particular theme as the result of a group process which transcends but includes the activity of each individual member. Discussion of this topic must be meeting some need in each individual member : it is also meeting a need belonging to the group as a whole, and helping to resolve some group tension. The temporary solution that it is providing may be a restrictive one, hampering the further progress of the group. Thus it may be reducing tension by diverting attention from some more sensitive area, enabling members to conceal differences that might become apparent were another topic to be discussed. Another diversion is the direction of criticism to persons not present in the group. The temptation to play some of the games described by Berne does not apply only to the mothers. These lay participants of the group can easily learn a few of the rules and some of the tricks in the game of psychiatry and then they have the power to drag the leader of the group into the by-play at their level. The following passages quoted from Berne will provide an illustration.

E : "I think it's some unconscious oral frustration that makes him act that way."

F : "You seem to have your aggressions so well sub-limated."

G : "That painting symbolises smearing to me."

H : "In my case, painting is trying to please my father."

A further example gives an illustration of what happens in some therapy groups where, whatever occurs, the same interpretation can be made to serve.

Black :   "Well, anyway, when we're silent nobody is play-ing games."

White :   "Silence itself may be a game."

Red :   "Nobody was playing games today."

White :   "But not playing games may itself be a game."

These games or pastimes might well be called "diversions" (with a double meaning of the word) and they allow the members of the group and the leader to evade an examination of the nature of their own involvement.

The group counsellor must be aware of these processes, but for her they do not have the same significance in themselves that they could have for a group psychotherapist. She is concerned with what goes on in the group in so far as it relates to her terms of reference, and she looks for its significance in terms of the mothers' interaction with their children. She may wonder, for example, whether the mothers who discuss their marital situation are feeling that they have been unjustly singled out to bear the burden of their respective family's difficulties. If she thinks that this is so, she may make some comment designed to help the mothers to express their feelings more directly, on the lines of "Perhaps we are feeling that the fathers ought to be here too". She does not say, "Perhaps Mrs. Smith is feeling . . .", singling out the most vocal member . . . but attributes the feeling to the group as a whole. By using the plural pronoun "we" she indicated that she associates herself with the mothers, and is not attributing more responsibility to them than to their absent husbands. By using the word "father" she underlines the fact that it is their relationships with their children that are at issue, and so she helps to relate the discussion to the specific focus of the group.

The group counsellor makes use of the individual relationship she has with every member of the group, and she also makes use of the relationship which she has with the group as a whole. Her relationship with each member at an individual level cannot be ignored; she must be aware of it, and at times may have to direct her intervention to one particular person in the group. For example, if one mother remains silent, and appears to feel isolated from the others, the group counsellor might wish to respond to her silent presence in some particular way. The group counsellor might also think it sometimes appropriate to give some personal attention to an over-talkative "monopolist" who is holding up the progress of the group. The behaviour of both these members, however, is also part of a total group process in which all are implicated, and the group counsellor might find ways of helping the individuals through intervention at a group level, and in this way avoid the risk of weakening the group, and of hindering the development of its capacity to solve its own problems. In the same way that the social worker, in an individual interview, identifies the needs of her client and responds to them, so the group counsellor needs to identify and respond to the needs of the group as a whole.

Suppose that in our group of mothers, one mother were to complain forcefully that the treatment is a waste of time and that the group counsellor is not giving her any help. Suppose that the other mothers allow her to speak but remain silent themselves. In any treatment situation, the expression of existing negative feelings can have value. Many patients or clients, however, while experiencing feelings of hostility, may fear to show them, and others may have to pretend, even to themselves, that these feelings do not exist. The angry mother in the group is verbalising feelings that all to some extent share, but only she is able to acknowledge and, furthermore, express. She is acting as spokesman for the group. The group counsellor can respond directly to this mother, accepting her hostility, and demonstrating that angry feelings are present in every relationship and that their presence can be acknowledged without harm. This would be appropriate in an individual situation, but to do this in a group would isolate the angry mother from the rest of the group and leave the unexpressed hostility unrecognised, perhaps by implication making it into something even more dangerous. What is needed from the group counsellor is a group response, an acceptance of the hostility as something offered by the whole group, and an underlining of the point that her relationship, which can absorb the anger without being damaged, is with the whole group. It is in this way that the group counsellor is able to make contact with a wider range of feelings in her clients than would be possible in individual work, since feelings which would not be expressed in an individual interview can achieve indirect and vicarious expression through the activities of a group.

Some of the group counsellor's interventions will include interpretations stimulated by particular events in the group but related to types of behaviour in general. The group counsellor coming fresh to the group process need not feel that her interpretations should match those of her mentors, tutors, or supervisors, or, for that matter, the authors of this book. Every interpretation is part of the interaction between her and the group members, her own experience and her own personality are part of that interaction, and the interpretation is her own personal and professional response to the immediate situation. The question is not whether an interpretation is right or wrong, but whether it is appropriate, taking all these factors into account. In all groups some interpretations are noted by the leader but stored away in his mind and not used at the time. Some interpretations will not occur to the leader until long afterwards, and then they will form part of his own personal and professional development, if not of the group's. In this sense one need never regret the afterthought "Why didn't I say that . . .?", because the particular thought will become embodied in what the leader has to offer to subsequent groups.

Let us now look at an extract from an actual record of a counselling group. This group, which was led by a psychiatric social worker, met in the psychiatric department of a children's hospital. It was composed of mothers whose children had been referred because of asthma, and the children were receiving treatment from a child psychiatrist in a parallel group. The two groups were seen as complementary to each other. In this counselling group, a common concern of the mothers was with their children's group treatment; and the focus of the group was upon the mothers' relationships with their children, in the special circumstances caused by the children's illness, and in the current treatment situation. The aim of the group coun-sellor had two aspects. In general, she set out to augment the help given to the children by affecting the relationship between them and their mothers; more specifically, she wished to help the mothers to express more easily their reactions to the difficulties and frustrations of their situation, and their mixed feelings at being in a position in which they had to accept help from others.

This was the third meeting of the group, and five mothers were present.

Mrs. C started talking as soon as everyone had sat down. She described how she had taken her son to the local authority child welfare clinic to be immunised against polio, and a woman medical officer had refused to immunise him because he was wheezing slightly. The doctor's manner was felt by Mrs. C to be critical and unsympathetic, and, furthermore, the doctor had discussed asthma in the child's presence, something which Mrs. C had always tried to avoid herself. Mrs. C was agitated while recounting this, she flushed and stammered, and her eyes filled with tears. The other members of the group all sympathised warmly with her, and spoke very critically about the behaviour of the woman doctor. Mrs. H and Mrs. Y said that they would not allow such a woman to see their children again if they were Mrs. C, and that they would have told her exactly how they felt. Mrs. C said that she had felt very angry, and would have liked to express this, but "I never can, I always have an inhibition about it". She wished she could express her feelings more easily, in the way that other people seemed able to do. The discussion remained lively and heated, as the mothers talked of the difficulty of knowing what they should do in situations were medical opinion is not unanimous; for example, some doctors advocate immunisation against polio for asthmatic children, and some doctors advise against it.

Mrs. Y then asked the group counsellor for direct advice about her boy's nail-biting. The books on psychology that she had consulted told her to ignore it, and she had tried to do this but had had no success; her boy was now biting his nails more than ever. The group counsellor said that there seemed to be a feeling that it was no good looking for help from experts, as they did not even agree among themselves, and that psychology was not much help either. Perhaps they were wondering about her, and whether she would be able to give them any help. This was greeted with a short silence, and then Mrs. Y denied that she had meant to be critical of psychology, citing at length the number of books on psychology that she had read. She went on to criticise the staff at her son's school for their handling of him. They made little attempt to understand his problems. She found it impossible to tell his teacher how she felt. The other mothers all agreed that they could not talk to their children's teachers either; and they went on to speak of women teachers as dangerous and powerful figures who needed to be placated, and who might make trouble for people they did not like. The mothers were all in agreement that it was important to appear pleasant and grateful in front of the teachers, and to hide any angry feelings they might have. Mrs. B, whose child attended a special, open-air school, made an exception for one teacher there; this teacher was a married woman, herself the mother of an asthmatic child, and she therefore understood about the difficulties. The other mothers said they wished their children could have such a teacher. The group counsellor said that it was understandable that they could feel that another woman with a child with asthma was, in a sense, in the same group that they were in. She went on to say that they seemed to feel that teachers, and the staff of clinics and hospitals, who had not got the same direct experience of their difficulties, would be likely to blame and criticise them.

Mrs. Y said that the doctors at the hospital, "and I don't mean you", did not seem to understand how much the mothers wanted to be told about their children's illnesses, and to receive direct advice. Several of the others agreed. Mrs. H then said to the group counsellor that she wished that "someone like you" would go to her son's school and explain about his illness and the difficulties that it caused. Mrs. C described her son's demanding behaviour, how he insisted upon having his own way, and how he always seemed to have an attack of asthma if she did not give in to him. Mrs. H and Mrs. C described similar episodes involving their children, and said the children's inability to tolerate any frustration meant that they had no friends, as other children did not want to play with them. Only Mrs. B, who had hardly spoken hitherto, and who was the only mother in the group whose child was a girl, said complacently that she did not have this problem with Jacqueline. The other four mothers then vied with each other in giving examples of the ways in which their boys tried to dominate them, and get their own way in every situation. The mothers spoke of this behaviour as something abnormal, and they strongly approved a firm attitude on the part of parents and of school teachers. Mrs. Y said she had been very relieved when Dr. S (the child psychiatrist) had told her that it was all right to smack Richard. Before leaving, the mothers asked in some detail about the arrangements for the next session. The group counsellor indicated that she would be looking forward to seeing them all again next week.

Reading through this record, one finds a single major theme predominating. Throughout the session, the mothers seemed to be preoccupied with their feelings towards those people who were professionally concerned with the health, welfare, or education of themselves or of their children. In the immediate situation, these people were assumed by the group counsellor to be representative of herself.

This theme needs to be studied at two levels. First of all, at the individual level, there is the meaning that this theme has to each of the mothers in terms of her own personal needs and her current life. Secondly, at the group level, there is the importance of the theme as an expression of the current situation in the group, and the contribution it makes to the solution of the problems posed by the juxtaposition of cohesive and disruptive forces.

It appears that the mothers anticipated that "the experts" would criticise and blame them. It could be assumed that this anticipation was connected with the feelings which they had about their children's illnesses, and the degree to which they felt responsible for them. It could also be connected with the anger and resentment which they felt at the burdens which they had to carry, these feelings co-existing with their love and concern for their children. Not only did they appear to anticipate a punitive reaction, but their behaviour seemed actually designed to provoke this as if it were what they sought. If the group counsellor were to react in a way that could be interpreted as unsympathetic or repressive, their already-existing feelings of hostility would be legitimised, and a scapegoat found to take the blame for continuing difficulties.

The behaviour of the mothers in the group also needs to be considered as a product of their experience of the parent–child relationship, containing something from their experiences as children in relation to their own parents, and also something of their self-image of themselves as parents in relation to their own children. The group counsellor made no reference to this, although it might well have been a theme of individual casework.

At the level of group interaction, the record shows an attempt to form an in-group consisting inclusively and exclusively of mothers with asthmatic children. Everyone not in this in-group was seen as unsympathetic. This served to ensure sufficient cohesiveness for the time being, and it also helped to contain the urge to compete for the individual attention of the group counsellor, which might have disrupted the group. It also diverted atention from individual problems and allowed responsibility to be attributed elsewhere. But, at the same time, the presence of the group counsellor aroused considerable anxiety, and her relative passivity provoked fears of retaliation and wishes for firmer control.

The first recorded contribution of the group counsellor was a comment on the mothers' criticism of the behaviour of the woman medical officer, an interpretation at a conscious or near-conscious level that attempted to link the description of an outside event, and their reactions to it, with their relationship to her in the group. The purpose of this comment was to help the mothers to express their feelings more openly, to encourage a more direct consideration of significant relationships, and to help the group to find a less restricting solution to its current problem. This intervention on the part of the group counsellor seems to have been premature; at this stage it was too direct and too personal, focusing upon an area which they were not yet ready to consider. The covert attacks on her continued and became more specific, this time displaced on to the teachers, and fears of retaliation were indicated. The next comment made by the group counsellor was more cautious, and was designed to show that she was aware of the hostile feelings without being afraid of them, and without losing sight of the difficulties which had brought the mothers together, and which were real. After this the criticism shifted from the teachers to hospital personnel, and an inclination to test out the group counsellor's sincerity and capacity to help was shown. There was an apparent change of topic when they started to talk about their children's behaviour, but it seemed as if they were also talking about their own behaviour. While they discussed their children they were, at the same time, revealing their own fears of having overstepped the limit, their anxieties at the permissive behaviour of the group counsellor, and their fears that she might retaliate. Before they left they needed to be reassured that they would be welcome at the following session.

Two further points need to be mentioned. This record illustrates the way in which all the different personal relationships that an individual makes can be considered as related to each other, so that each forms part of an interlocking system or network. This system is in a perpetual state of adjustment and change, as an alteration in one relationship will have an effect upon all the others. Thus the mothers in the group could move from discussing their reactions to the doctor in the child welfare clinic, to the teachers, to the hospital doctors,

illustrating throughout this their reactions to the group counsellor. They could describe their feelings about their children's
behaviour in such a way, and in such a context, that it could
be treated as illustrating their view of the group counsellor's
relationship with themselves. Thus no single relationship which
might be demonstrated in the mothers' behaviour or described
in their verbal interchanges could be evaluated or understood
in isolation; each had to be considered as a fragment of an
inter-related whole, and intervention at any one point could
be used to influence the whole field.

The second point concerns the treatment of the material
provided in this session as if it were the production of a single
entity. It is important to emphasise again that attitudes and
feelings attributed to the group as such are not identical with
the attitudes and feelings of each individual member. The
hostility shown towards the group counsellor has been considered as an attribute of the group as a whole, contributing
to the temporary solution of a problem also belonging to the
whole group. To the establishment of this group solution each
of the individual members made some contribution. At an
individual level, this pattern of behaviour in the group must
have had some particular meaning for each of the mothers
present: for Mrs. C, whose frustration at being unable to
express her angry feelings about people in authority began
the session; for Mrs. Y, who vigorously developed this theme;
for Mrs. B, who indicated through her complacency the
satisfaction which she derived as a spectator rather than as
an active participant. Though each member would have a
different individual attitude from that of the group counsellor,
the hostility could be treated as a common denominator. It
had a meaning for each one within this particular context,
and, therefore, a point was provided at which an intervention
affecting the total group processes could be made.

Up to now, we have been discussing Group Counselling
mainly in relation to social work, and have taken our examples
from groups of mothers conducted by psychiatric social workers

in child guidance and child psychiatric clinics; we have also included an example from a similar group led by a psychiatrist. It is in such groups that the essential characteristics of Group Counselling can be most clearly seen. Here it can be demonstrated that the members of the group are not psychotherapy patients but have a different commitment and different expectations; that their personal problems are only relevant at the point where they impinge on the problems on which the group is focused; that intervention takes place in the area of interpersonal relationships; and that the skilled use of relationships is a primary part of the group counselling process.

Examples from other contexts must also be considered. The contexts are important. Group Counselling is more diverse and is influenced to a greater extent by its setting than is Group Psychotherapy. To some extent it is the setting that determines the aims and supplies the focus of the counselling group.

A different example of an agency in which group work may take place is found in a probation department. In this setting, probation officers sometimes conduct groups with boys who are referred to them by the Courts. Such boys come from different backgrounds and have different motivations; they have in common the fact that they have broken some law and that this has led to the making of a probation order. The probation officer will have to elaborate this common factor, or establish some additional and more specific basis for selection if he is to find the focus that is necessary for Group Counselling and avoid the hazards of unstructured group work in the no-man's land that is neither counselling nor psychotherapy. Attempts are sometimes made to offer a partial explanation for delinquent behaviour in terms of a failure to identify with an authority figure and therefore a concomitant failure to incorporate acceptable standards and modes of behaviour. In this sense, delinquency is not something that has gone wrong, but is a deficiency in the provisions that are necessary for development to proceed normally. It is what has not gone right. Such an assumption is one of many that could be used to provide a starting point and a focus for a counselling group : it enables us to discuss the role of group leader by means of a string of further assumptions. The authors are not probation officers, and these are our phantasies for what they are worth. Probation officers would have the right to disclaim the validity of what follows.

We imagine the group leader accepting the focus that we have suggested for him, and selecting the members of his group carefully on this basis. He will consider the relationship between himself and the group in the light of the deficiency in normal provision that has been assumed, and which he hopes to do something to remedy. Whatever other feelings are transferred to him, he will also inevitably represent that authority, parental, educational, or magisterial, with which his probationers have had their difficulties in the past. They now have an opportunity to enter into a fresh relationship with an authority figure in the context of a peer group.

The leader will perhaps hope that through the use of group, rather than individual, methods he can facilitate and expedite the open expression of feelings and attitudes, and enable the group members to test out the limits of the relationship that he is offering them. Phantasies will then be more quickly revealed for what they are, and strong feelings will become less frightening when known to be shared. He will be likely to take active steps to relate positively to the group, demonstrating his tolerance and his concern, and his capacity to remain undamaged by overt and covert hostility.

Within this framework, he will need to keep anxiety within the limits of the group's capacity to tolerate it at any moment of time. He will expect to see an increase in this capacity, and hope that the group will develop sufficient strength and cohesion to take over some of this responsibility for itself. He may then think it appropriate to introduce certain experiences into the group sessions in order to augment their impact and increase the focus upon the areas he considers most relevant.

One such experience might be an exposure to the demands of authority. In this way the boys would be given an opportunity to develop new ways of dealing with the challenges they have been unable to deal with successfully in real life situations.

Elsewhere, mention has been made of a counselling group composed of patients discharged to the community after long periods in a mental hospital, suggesting such a group as a means by which the support derived from living in a protective environment might be extended into the community. This provides us with an example of a counselling group in a different setting, and focused upon different aims. If we look for a relationship, significant to all its members, on which this group could focus, we do not find it in that between parent and child, nor between youth and authority. We postulate two sets of relevant relationships : there is the relationship that exists between each patient and the mental hospital on the one hand, and that between the patient and the outside community on the other hand. The group counsellor may be identified with either hospital or community—indeed, one of these organisations may be his employing authority—but in the group he needs to represent both, and to make a link between the two.

The leader will have to limit the amount of stress within the group, and keep it within the tolerance of individual members who may be exceptionally vulnerable. He may have to play an active role to meet individual and group needs, which could include a need to experience continued dependence and protection. Indeed, it may take time for such a cluster to develop into a counselling group. Given sufficient time, participation in this group may be expected to provide some sense of comfort and security, to reduce the feelings of alienation and stigma, and to provide experience in relating to other people within a safe environment; it may go on to extend the range of responses that are available to the members for meeting challenging situations.

We have envisaged these last two groups as being led by

social workers, who may have had some specific training in group work, or who may be transferring concepts derived from work with individuals to a group setting. Group coun- sellors are not drawn only from social workers. Groups of comparable composition to those conducted by probation officers, and designed to serve similar ends, may be found in approved schools; here they may be conducted by psychologist, teacher, or doctor. Groups of mental hospital patients are sometimes led by a nurse, a hospital chaplain, a doctor, or a social worker, singly or in any combination. Thus in these and other institutions, staff who have no relevant group work train- ing within their own professional framework are expected to take part in group work, or they may choose to do so. Many other examples may be found. There are special schools where teaching the children can merge into counselling, and where more formal counselling may be necessary for groups of children or of parents. Prisons have their need for group counselling at different levels, and here the leaders of groups might be prison staff, staff specially appointed for the purpose, visiting specialists coming in from outside, or any combination of the three. The use of visiting specialists has its justification, but care needs to be taken to avoid fragmentation of the activities for which the different categories of staff have to take responsibility. The staff of an institution cannot expect to hand over to outsiders the responsibility for dealing with the emotional problems that life in the institution engenders. It could be argued that in each special situation the initiator and leader of the group activity should come from the profes- sion which is primarily concerned with the setting in which the group work takes place.

There are many other examples where fields of work, which properly belong to an established profession, bring emotional problems to light, and these have to be faced and cannot be denied or warded off. This is particularly true for those professions whose consumers experience anxiety about the nature of the service which they are receiving, and about its consequences. Here again it is not possible or desirable always to call in an outside expert to deal with the emotional difficulties which are revealed, and which present problems, in other people's jobs. Many professional workers will rather see this as part of their own responsibility, and will elect to deal with it themselves. These workers need to have an opportunity to extend and enrich their techniques with some of the concepts we have been describing as part of Group Counselling. Just as social work has borrowed concepts from psychotherapy, and Group Counselling from Group Psychotherapy, so other disciplines can borrow from Group Counselling. There are many situations outside structured group work where a doctor, nurse, psychologist, health visitor, or teacher meets groups of people in connection with some aspect of his own work and has to interpret[1] to them their expectations of one another and the possible outcomes of his techniques. He needs to enrich these discussions with knowledge of his own involvement in the group processes. He has to have some idea of the hidden questions behind the questions he is asked, and of the alternative meanings of the answers that he gives. He needs to be able to draw comparisons, to detect common themes, and to recognise and deal with some of the anxieties that will be only marginally expressed. He needs to be able to answer question with question, so as to extend rather than contract the area of discussion. All this involves the application of techniques which have been developed in Group Counselling and in casework. This does not make him into a caseworker, and casework is not the primary object of the exercise. If he can benefit by learning something about Group Counselling

---

[1] It will be observed that we have used the word "interpret" in the above passage. We have done this deliberately. We do not consider that the process of interpretation should be considered the prerogative of the psychotherapist and the social worker, even though these two professions use interpretation in a special and disciplined way.

methods, it is not in order to give him an additional profession
but to make him more competent in dealing with some of the
issues in his own. Any skill he acquires must become built into
his individual personal style, and become part of the practice
of his own profession.

CHAPTER 7

Group Discussion

In turning to Group Discussion, we turn away from the field of psychotherapy and counselling, from concern with personal problems and with family difficulties, to the field of education and to concern with problems of teaching and of learning. I would be misleading if we were to think of Group Discussion as a half-way house, placed somewhere between psychotherapy and education. The purpose of Group Discussion is always related to education, and, in distinction to the other two group systems, it must always remain within the limits appropriate to a method of education. It is, however, a very special method, a method which makes use of concepts of dynamic group behaviour and insights derived from Group Psychotherapy and Group Counselling, and which shares some part of their aims and methods. At one and the same time, it seeks to promote intellectual and emotional growth.

Brief reference has already been made to Group Discussion in order to account for its inclusion in this study, and in order to outline the features which we consider the three systems to have in common. In Group Discussion, we should expect once again to find a model containing the physical characteristics of the basic group situation such as we have described: a number of people sitting together in a circle, with a leader and engaging in "free" discussion. In practice, we find that this model can be considerably modified, and that it is not impossible for the principles of Group Discussion to be applied to larger groups meeting for a common learning purpose in

110

class or conference, even when these physical characteristics are absent. Although it is usually thought preferable to divide large conferences into a number of sub-groups for discussion, in order to retain something of the intimate pattern of the original model, it is not beyond possibility to conduct Group Discussion in a classroom setting for thirty, forty, or an even larger membership. The example given in detail later in this chapter is taken from such a situation. We would not wish to suggest that a group of this size is either typical or ideal— but the process of Group Discussion can simultaneously engage a larger number of people than could either Group Psycho-therapy or Group Counselling.

In Group Discussion, as in the other two systems, we should also expect to find attempts to promote that positive group development, that active involvement on the part of individual members, which can bring with it the possibility of personal growth and change. The freedom of discussion, again, is made possible through the existence of a definite but implicit bargain between members and leader. But since the purpose of the group is not psychotherapy, or counselling, but education, the members of the group are not patients or clients, but students. They have not come for help with difficulties of personality or of relationships; they have come to learn. The participants may be students for the limited period of a one-day conference or they may be enrolled on a prolonged professional training course. Difficulties can occur with mature students with some previous experience of the subject which is being discussed. They may have engaged in the role of student, but they may have come with the clear intention of teaching. Whether the intentions are fully acknowledged or not, those who come to teach and those who come to learn may frequently find themselves reversing their roles.

Members of a discussion group are not prepared, nor are they expected, to expose either their total personalities or an area of specific personal difficulty in the group. The bargain

between members and leader must therefore include an understanding on the part of the leader that he is not to treat them
as patients or clients; that when aspects of individual psychopathologies are inevitably revealed in the group, he will pay
no open attention to them; and, when problems are exposed,
neither personal comment nor even a change in the procedure
will follow. Should it become clear that any member of the
group is seeking personal help of which he is in need, the
leader would not attempt to use the group as a therapeutic
agent. However, he might, if approached, offer such a member
an individual interview in order to discuss the possibility of
referring him for help elsewhere. Group Discussion may also
be a group system which aims to promote change in individual
members, but such change does not occur as the result of any
therapeutic endeavour : rather, it is the result of the members'
exposure to a learning process of a very particular kind.

Earlier in this book, mention has also been made of
the individual supervision process as studied and described by
caseworkers in particular. While this provides some pointers
for the student of Group Discussion, its application is so much
narrower and more specific that it cannot furnish in any way
an exact parallel. The use of Group Discussion methods
now extends beyond the field of professional education and
disciplined learning. Nevertheless, some lessons can be drawn
from the ways in which supervisors may help students to
understand and modify their own part in a two-way relationship, while, at the same time, the supervisors refrain from
intruding into the students' personal lives.

These previous references to Group Discussion must
now be expanded and qualified; its relationship, on the one
hand to Group Psychotherapy and Group Counselling, on
the other hand to other methods of education, must be
made clear and the role of the leader must be described and
illustrated.

The participants in a discussion group have come to learn,
and they have come to learn something which cannot be fully

provided by academic methods of teaching or through participation at an intellectual level alone. It could be said that one
of the principal things that they have come to learn is to
understand and express the feelings which they experience in
any task in which the techniques involve the use of their own
personalities. This task may be a specific one. Where Group
Discussion takes place in a professional setting, the task will
be concerned with the provision of an individual service or
material to patients, clients, or customers, or it will involve
working as a member of a team in a work situation. All these
activities involve the use of personal relationships, of some
sort, in some degree. In other situations the task may be a
more personal one, though still contained within an educational framework; it may be concerned with the entry into
adult life, with the assumption of new responsibilities, or with
the preparation for some particular period of stress. In any of
these examples, the aim of Group Discussion will be to widen
the capacity of each individual member to use his own
personality in each various enterprise or living activity.

There are some learning situations, some professional train-
ings, and some tasks and enterprises where the relevance of
an individual's capacity to make appropriate and effective use
of his own personality is clearly seen.

Thus, at a conference of marriage guidance counsellors, the
question was asked, "What does a psychiatrist do?" The
questioner added, "I know that a surgeon uses the knife, a
physician uses drugs, but what does a psychiatrist use?"

The answer, which had to be built up gradually, ran like
this. "The surgeon uses his knife, but he also uses his personality.
He uses his knife scientifically, but he uses his self unscientifically even if he uses it effectively. The physician uses his
drugs scientifically, but he uses his self unscientifically. The
psychiatrist (though not the psychiatrist of every school) has
nothing to use but his own self, but there is this difference;
he uses his own self scientifically."

The social worker shares with the psychiatrist in the use

of concepts which have been developed in order to use the self as a professional tool. In these two professions it has long been taken for granted that the relationship between the professional worker and the patient or client is a major factor in the helping process and that it is necessary to make it a subject for study from both ends. Any social worker, for example, even when he is dealing with some concrete practical difficulty and using well-recognised techniques, has to be aware not only of his client's complex emotional responses but also of his own. Where there is a selection procedure for membership of branches of these two professions, flexibility and a capacity for personal growth and development are stressed as desirable qualities. During training, the student is encouraged to develop his own self-awareness and sensitivity. It is recognised that this is a part of the professional training that cannot be provided through academic lectures or the reading of textbooks alone. Well-established teaching methods that attempt to provide it include Group Discussion as well as individual supervision focused upon on-going professional work or on more general problems. In addition, for some fields of work a training analysis is advocated, but the consideration of this falls outside the scope of this book.

In the training of those who wish to become leaders of groups themselves, Group Discussion must play an essential part. It alone provides an experience which can help them to understand their own feelings and reactions in a group, as well as to identify group processes, and it can give a living example of the way in which a leader may make use of these processes to further the particular aims of the group.

But an interest in the professional relationship and an appreciation of its importance is not, as we have seen, now confined to psychiatry and social work. The same component, involving the use of the self, is present, though often less well recognised, in many other activities. It is acknowledged in the rules and customs, sometimes unwritten and even unspoken, which exist in many professions and occupations to govern relationships between those providing and those receiving a service; between doctor and patient, solicitor and client, sales representative and customer. Even where it is not considered a specific part of the professional process, there is an ever-increasing realisation that the interpersonal relationship through which the professional help is given occupies a central position and can help or hinder the worker's use of occupational skills and the client's readiness to profit by them. This applies particularly to all transactions where help is offered through a face-to-face meeting, and concerns such professions as medicine, nursing, teaching, and the Church, among others. In these professions there is an active demand for an extension of training to include an understanding of human relationships over and above anything which can be derived from academic lectures in psychology. It may be that the skills that are being sought are those of a caseworker or a group counsellor, but the methods by which these skills are imparted are the methods of Group Discussion. Information provided through lectures can be absorbed at an intellectual level without being converted into increased insight into the behaviour of oneself and others, and may even defeat its own purpose, becoming encapsulated and divorced from everyday experience. Students need to participate actively in this learning process and relate it directly to their own experience if it is not to become a barrier rather than a stepping-stone to further progress.

Another field in which group methods are sometimes used is found in the in-service training programmes in industry. Here there is not the same focus upon the use of a particular professional relationship, but rather a recognition of the importance of an individual's behaviour as a member of a team and as colleague, supervisor, manager, and subordinate. There is also concern with the capacity of individuals to absorb change, in a field where organisational and tech-nological developments often take place rapidly. The readiness and competence of an individual to alter habitual ways of behaviour, and to accept changes in the organisation around him, depends upon much more than an intellectual comprehension of the situation; it can involve such additional factors as his sense of security, his ability to trust others, and the nature and depth of the satisfactions that he derives from his work. Here intellectual methods of training and retraining, such as the didactic lecture, have proved inadequate; indeed, they may have hazards as well as limitations. For example, a lecture describing and advocating new methods of working may be seen as a concealed attack on existing methods and on their operators, who will thus be stimulated to resist the proposed changes. Alternatively, it may serve to change the workers' image of themselves and the work they are doing, providing an illusion that something is different, without producing any actual, appreciable change in the methods of operation. The illusion satisfies their ambitions and so makes further effort unnecessary.

In this dilemma, industry has turned to dynamic group psychology, and has adopted group methods, known in this context as "T-groups". By this means the advocates of group methods hope that more fundamental changes in attitudes and behaviour patterns can be produced. It is anticipated that an increase in sensitivity and self-awareness resulting from an exposure to group interaction will reduce dependence upon stereotyped, habitual modes of behaviour, and that there will be an increase in flexibility and in readiness to experiment as a result. A T-group may be composed of a number of people unknown to each other and drawn from different industrial settings. Alternatively, firms may set up their own T-groups as part of an internal in-service training programme, despite the complications that could be caused by the prior acquaintanceship and the hierarchical relationships of the people concerned. In each T-group there will be one, or perhaps two, group leaders who are known as "trainers". The trainer encourages the group to focus upon its own behaviour in a deliberately unstructured and leaderless situation, in which the old landmarks and familiar roles that the members habitually make use of are missing or are no longer effective.

It has been suggested by one writer[1] that the difference between a T-group and a psychotherapeutic group is to be found partly in the different composition, T-group members having more adequate defences than patients in a psychotherapeutic group, and partly in the different sets of expectations brought to these groups by their members. These distinctions may be valid. However, it may be thought that these circumstances are not enough in themselves to account for all the differences, nor can they be relied upon to provide sufficient safeguards. The inadequacy of certain defences may be discovered too late, and expectations may not be fulfilled unless they are shared and respected.

The authors have no personal experience of these groups, but it would appear to them that the T-group is designed primarily to be of benefit to the organisation that sponsors it, and only indirectly for the benefit of the group itself and its individual members. Traditionally, it has not been thought necessary to give consideration to those who have to leave a post in industry because of inadequacy revealed through the stresses of new demands and the strains of interacting personalities. The use of group methods, in which such stresses and strains may be deliberately introduced, creates new hazards. This gives added emphasis to the importance that we attach to seeing that the aims and limitations of a T-group, and the sanction that is given to the leader by the group, should be formulated and understood as clearly as possible. It should remain the responsibility of the leader of the T-group, as of all discussion groups, to see that the defences of individual members are in fact adequate (this cannot be safely assumed), and that the stress that is inevitable in such a situation is kept within the tolerance of the most vulnerable member. Responsibility should also be taken for any casualties of the group.

[1] T. Johns, T-Group traumas, *Journal of Institute of Personnel Management*, Vol. I, No. 7, 1968.

This is a consideration that does not apply to industry alone. By the same token, educational establishments have some responsibility for the students whom they select or accept for a training course in which group methods are used such that the vulnerable parts of the personality may become revealed. If any of these students have to withdraw from the course, responsibility remains with the educational establishment, and attempts should be made to secure appropriate help for them.

Professional and occupational training of one sort or another is not the only field in which Group Discussion methods may be used; they are equally applicable wherever an understanding of human behaviour is involved in the subject at issue. Group Discussion, for example, may be offered to young people in school or youth club as part of a programme of preparation for adult life and as a way of giving help with the difficulties of this particular transitional stage. Adaptation to the challenges and opportunities of each successive stage in life, whether of leaving school, of marriage, childbirth, and the parental problems of child rearing, of retirement and old age, can also be looked upon as a task for which preparation is possible, and in which different areas and levels of the personality are involved. These problems are general rather than specific, anticipated rather than actual. Were they specific and actual, the group discussants might come instead as clients to counsellors, selecting a particular agency, accepting a different status, and anticipating a different process.

In schools and youth clubs, the adoption of Group Discussion methods has come with the realisation that instruction in the physical facts of sexual behaviour, coupled perhaps with moral precepts, is not an adequate way of meeting young people's needs. Sexual behaviour, it is now thought, needs to be included within the broad context of human relationships, and is by no means the only preoccupation in this area; other relationships, such as those with parents, siblings, peer group, and people in authority, also need to be included. Any such attempt at education in human relationships, if it is not to be sterile, must be linked with the actual experiences that the young people have and the situations that most closely concern them, and must involve them as active participants in the process.

We have considered some different learning situations to which the methods of Group Discussion can be applied. We now need to make a more detailed examination of these methods, and of the underlying process that all discussion groups have in common. Whereas Group Psychotherapy has no directed focus and Group Counselling is focused upon a particular problem or a particular difficulty in relationships, Group Discussion is focused at any one time upon a theme or topic. These themes or topics will be of particular interest to all the members of the group and form the basis which they have in common. This is, of course, also true of groups which meet to discuss such topics as the origins of the solar system or the behaviour of the common earthworm. But these are topics which can be treated as external to the discussants.[1]

The topics of Group Discussion, in our meaning of the term, cannot remain external to the discussants. They may be dependent upon factual information, but they are also concerned with personal relationships. Therefore relationships in the group itself, and the behaviour of individual members, will exemplify what is being discussed. The members of the group are observers, but they also form part of the field that is being observed. It is in this respect that an essential difference between Group Discussion and other forms of education lies. It is because of this that the experience cannot be one that is exclusively intellectual. No member can escape involvement in the group as well as in the topic.

The leader then has a delicate task, and a task that differs

[1] In fact, in some circumstances these topics too may not be without emotional impact. Galileo went to the stake for challenging established ideas about the solar system, and the topic of the earthworm was used by Darwin.

in some important respects from that of a group psycho-therapist or a group counsellor. He must try to maximise the effectiveness of the group as a means of teaching members about human behaviour, including their own and his own. He must enable all members to participate in the group, to contribute from their own experience, and to see the relevance of the topic to their own situation. He must help them to study their own attitudes and behaviour and those of others, to question them and to seek to understand them. He must at the same time contain the experience within an educational framework, and within the limits of what has been sanctioned.

The group, as we have seen, will be focused upon a particular theme. The same theme may continue throughout a series of meetings, or the members may choose a different theme for each meeting, or a number of themes may have to be dealt with to meet the requirements of a particular syllabus. This theme will be concerned with some aspect of human relationships. In a group composed of caseworkers, for example, different situations containing casework problems of particular interest or difficulty may be illustrated and discussed. In a group of general practitioners, the relationship between doctor and patient may be considered. A group of school leavers may choose, as their theme, relationships between young people and their elders, or may be concerned with such particular problems as drug addiction or delinquency. These are all themes which have many different aspects and which can be approached in different ways and considered at different levels. They can be related on one level to different systems of thought. To the individual student, a particular theme will have both its academic and its practical aspect, and he will bring to it theoretical and conventional viewpoints and, at another level, attitudes based upon personal prejudge-ments. All these different aspects can provide material for discussion and it is the leader's job to draw out this material and to make it available to the group. He must see that the theme is discussed as widely and on as many levels as possible.

This particular skill of a Group Discussion leader can be briefly described as making appropriate links and pointing out relevant connections and resemblances. In relating together all these contributions, individual and corporate, verbal and non-verbal, and showing the relevance that each one has to the topic, he has to construct a framework. This framework is his own contribution. Value is given to every other contribution as the leader takes it, accepts it, adds to it, or adjusts it, and places it within the framework.

The different aspects of the theme that could relate to each other will depend upon the richness and variety of the material that the members of the group, including the leader, are able to provide, individually and corporately. The leader may choose to point out to the group such connections as he is able to discern between the topics under discussion, the contributions of each individual member, and the behaviour of the group as a whole. He may relate attitudes expressed directly or indirectly in the group, and attitudes attributed to others outside the group. He may relate theoretical knowledge and personal experience. He may use behaviour that takes place inside the group to throw light on behaviour outside the group. He may introduce fresh concepts himself, linking present experiences with different scientific systems, such as anthropology, sociology, or psychoanalysis, in order to stimulate alternative ways of thinking and to elicit new material. In this way he also increases the capacity of members to see the same problem at a number of different levels at the same moment.

Many of the topics that are dealt with in Group Discussion depend upon factual information, but they are all also related to basic personal attitudes. These two aspects are complementary to each other and of equal importance; both need to be brought out. Unless relevant personal attitudes can be discussed with some openness, the proceedings of the group are likely to remain sterile and unproductive, and allow little room for development and change to take place at any level. There are various impediments to such free discussion which may be present; some of them, common to the three group systems, have already been mentioned. There is the widespread tendency towards concealment in which most of us share, a reluctance to expose our true feelings to others for fear of what might be revealed. There is an unwillingness to question standards and beliefs which have proved of value in the past, and in which much may have been invested. Furthermore, many discussion groups are held under the auspices of organisations which embody some authoritarian function, or are known or believed to endorse some particular line—such organisations as university, training body, school, or church, for example. Members of the group may feel it is expedient to adhere to what they imagine to be the "party line", perhaps suggested to them by the nature of the training that is being offered or by the particular sponsorship of the sessions. Their educational experiences in the past may have led them to believe that this is the way to be considered a "good" student and win the approval of their teachers. For converse reasons, others may feel it incumbent upon them to oppose the "party line". But whether it is accepted or rejected, its real or imagined existence provides individual members with roles to play and so protects them from involvement at a more personal level, and from the possibility of personal change.

The leader, at the beginning of the course or at any subsequent stage, may have to take an active part to liberate the discussion from the repetition of textbook knowledge or other conventional opinions, or from an embargo on any exposure of personal feelings. This may be necessary in order to establish certain basic conditions without which Group Discussion cannot take place at all. Since this is a group situation, an understanding of the learning problems of each individual is not enough; the leader must also be able to relate them to the context of the group as a whole. In order to play his part effectively, appropriately, and economically, the leader must be able to discern the behaviour of the group and relate it to the total situation. He must try to identify the factors that are contributing to the development of cohesive and disruptive forces; he must see what is threatening the group and the individual members, and how both are reacting to the threat; and he must detect the way in which group processes are operating and the particular problems which they are trying to solve. Some areas which may be particularly relevant to an understanding of the behaviour of a discussion group are illustrated and discussed below. These include the influence on behaviour of the overall task which faces the group, the impact of the specific theme on which the session is focused, and the relationship between the leader and the rest of the group.

These aspects of Group Discussion are among the points that are illustrated in the following "approximate" verbatim record of one particular group. The record is approximate in that it was not recorded on tape but was taken down in shorthand by a secretary. The group was part of a course of in-service training undertaken by a number of mental welfare officers of considerable experience but without any previous formal training. They numbered about thirty and included both sexes, although men predominated. The course had a syllabus which dealt with human growth and development. At each meeting there was a lecture related to one part of this syllabus, and this was followed by a free discussion. On this particular occasion the formal topic was "Parental Rejection of the Infant", and the psychiatrist who delivered the lecture also conducted the group.

In previous courses, discussions of this topic had tended to concentrate on criticism or support of the scientific basis of Bowlby's formulation regarding the effect of an infant's separation from its mother. Members of the group would argue whether these concepts were "scientific" or not, and the discussion often remained at an abstract level. On this occasion, in the hope that it would stimulate a more spontaneous reaction to such an emotionally loaded topic, the group discussion leader prefaced his lecture by the reading of two news items from the popular press. One item had appeared that very morning, and had been seen by most members of the group in their respective papers. The other article, which had appeared a year earlier, was in the leader's collection of newspaper cuttings, and was fortunately to hand.

First Article

The 25-year-old mother of three children, Mrs. Y, wants to find a home for a fourth baby she is expecting in July.

She would not part with her seven-year-old son . . . or her three-year-old daughter . . . but she said last night: "I don't like babies. I think they are terrible things. They all scream their heads off."

Mrs. Y and her husband insist they could not afford another child. Their third child, a 21-month-old girl, is in the care of the . . . Council.

Mrs. Y said she had asked the Almoner at . . . Hospital if she could have the baby adopted. The Almoner replied that she was shocked but she would see what she could do.

"Later the hospital said they were not prepared to help me. We wrote to an evening paper to see if we could get help through its columns. We would like the child to go to a good home where there are no other children—to someone who deserves a child."

As Mrs. Y spoke, her two children remained in the room watching television. Amid all the questions and answers, they kept their eyes on the television set. But they know about the child to be born and have been told that it will have to be "given away" or they will not be able to have a holiday this year.

"Babies are a full-time job. Two are quite enough, and this house is not made for a big family. Big families cause squabbling, and the father goes off for a drink to get some peace", said Mrs. Y. "We are a very happy family and I do not want to have anything to spoil it."

Second Article

MRS. Y WANTS HER BABY BACK.

Decision to give child away regretted.

Mrs. Y, aged 26, the housewife who with her husband decided to give away their baby before the child was born, has refused to sign the adoption papers for the baby girl who is now with her prospective foster parents.

Mrs. Y said yesterday, "I never thought it would happen to me. But I keep on thinking about the baby and wishing I hadn't given it away. I can't sleep at night and I lie awake worrying whether she is all right. I suppose it is the mother instinct. After all, she is my own flesh and blood."

Discussion

Student A : Do you think that there is anything important or any problem in a child's phantasy and rejection of its parents? It is so common for children to believe in fairies and to weave tales about this.

Leader : It is not a problem. In fact it is almost inevitable. There is a stage in the phantasy life of the child which includes finding someone to idealise. I did not have time to mention some of the more pathological processes which take place. When a child over-idealises its real parents it may in fact be a bad thing. Some children so much want the idea that their parents are good parents that they have to find excuses for them if anything is wrong with them. You come across adult people who are full of self-recrimination. It is as if they are saying "I must be bad" in order that their parents could remain good.

Student B : Would you care to comment on the case of Mrs. Y as being relevant to this lecture?

Leader : I wonder if you would like to say what your feelings are.

Student B : I think she is a horror and she does not deserve that child.

Student C : I think her true feelings are those of rejection, but now she has seen what effect this has on people. She is trying to make some measure of atonement.

Student D : I think it was a natural rejection of the child, but now she has been separated from it she wants it back. Separation makes the heart grow fonder.

Student E : With the father just going into gaol and now she wants this child back, could this be a sign that the father was rejecting it?

Student F : I wonder if there was a rejected child in her family?

Student B : She would get quite a considerable amount of money from the press for her story.

Leader : I don't think the press pay for this sort of thing.

Student B : She wrote an article for a Sunday newspaper, "Why I want to give my baby away". She would have got about £500 for that.

Leader : I could be wrong about payment. But let us look at the levels at which it has been discussed. We have had questions of the mother's feelings, internal guilt, external pressure. I think we have to think of it from all these points of view. But there are people who have to make practical decisions. There was perhaps a mental health worker involved here. Would he ask about the consequences to the mother or to the child? And now there is the question of the press and of payment. Do you think this publicity was to the best advantage? Why was there a market for it?

Student G : Well, it's a unique case.

Student E : Mr. Y was said to be earning £15 a week.

Student H : I wonder where he comes into it?

Student F : In the first place he gave his consent quite willingly.

Student H : He left the decision to her.

Student L : She may be the dominating factor.

Student C : There are people who like to have all this publicity made about them. Exhibitionists.

Leader : Yes, the publicity may have done her good in satisfying some of her wishes. Let us leave her for a moment and ask in general why are such things given so much publicity.

Student F : Panders to the taste of the masses.

Leader : Then why have the masses got that particular taste to pander to?

Student H : There is a part of Mrs. Y in all of us.

Leader : Is it then because we ourselves have had at times the same feelings which she has dared to express?

Student B : Oh no, I don't think so.

Student D : Perhaps yes.

Student J : I think we are all angry about things which we might possibly have done ourselves.

Leader : I think we are angry about things which we wouldn't do because we have had the task of learning not to do them. We have learnt some self-control and expect ourselves to have moral and ethical standards. We all have to overcome strong feelings of anger and rivalry and learn to become decent citizens, and if we see some other person who has not learned to control these emotions we feel angry with them.

Student A : I sometimes wonder if these problems occurred a thousand years ago. In the old days there was no press.

Leader : In biblical days, Samuel was given as a baby to the priesthood, and Moses had to be separated from his mother, although in that case the mother managed to get back into the nursing situation.

Student F : I can remember a case just over four years ago where a mother had given her child to a film star and then, five or six years later, wanted her back. There was a lot of publicity about it, but everyone seemed to be on the mother's side.

Student C : I think this Y case has just been a racket. The woman, I will not call her lady, just went into it for financial gain.

Student D : I don't think so.

Student B : But she did write that story for the papers.

Student D : I do not see how she could plan such an eventuality while she was pregnant.

Leader : How would anybody know that this article would sell, and, if so, why?

Student C : Because it is sensational, it is news.

Leader : What makes it news?

Student K : Because people have a lot of feeling for the unborn child.

Student L : It appeals to the masses because at some stage we all have these feelings of rejection for children.

Student B : I cannot understand how a child could be unwanted. If so, what is human right, and why is there such a thing as a human right?

Leader : We are coming to the stage where it is possible to have a married life without children. Why do people nevertheless want children?

Student F : Natural instinct.

Student H : Projection of the parent's personality.

Student A : I wonder if there are more broken marriages without children than with?

Leader : We could check on that. Figures will be available. It might be very interesting to do so.

Student B : In the Y case, I still think she did it for financial gain.

Leader : Do you think people are angry with her because she made money in that way?

Student B : Yes.

Leader : Are we? Are we angry with her because of that?

Student C : No. Not angry, disgusted.

Leader : Why?

Student F : Because it cuts across our moral code.

Student H : Anyone could have to make the same decision.

Student A : Many people have given their children away.

Student H : Sometimes they are given away to Auntie.

Leader : And, in those circumstances, does it upset us?

Student G : No.

Student C : Well, it upsets me.

Leader : Supposing Mrs. Y had not existed and this person and situation had been drawn out of the mind of a dramatist, and we had gone to see the play. We might say that this was true to life or that it was not true to life. Would we be angry with the character and with the playwright?

(*A medley of different comments, some impossible to hear.*)

Student — : I cannot understand why she became pregnant.

Student — : Accidental.

Leader : There is a story about a man whose wife had had a number of children, and on the birth of the eleventh child he announced to his friends that he and his wife were not going to have any more. "But why not?" they asked him. "Well," said the man, "at last I've found out what has been causing it all."

(*Loud laughter*)

Student E (*to secretary*): Have you got that down?

Student A : Surely in these days of family planning she could have been educated enough to avoid having any more children if she did not want them?

Student H : Did she reject it or did the father?

Leader : I think it is clear that the mother needs understanding in her own right. As a person living as part of a community, we each have a right to have the standards of the community and we have just been voicing these standards now. If we are angry with her, we are angry as members of the community. But we are also mental health workers and so we have to consider Mrs. Y as a person with a need. How did she get into that state of mind? It may be that she has abnormal needs for the publicity involved in the situation. There are some people who are the epitome of some fundamental emotion or of some problem. She is expressing herself in this way, and in an exaggerated way she represents something in a large number of ordinary people. We may not be able to do anything for her but we still have the responsibility of asking why this happened to her. Up to now we have been ordinary people and we have been expressing ourselves as ordinary people. But we have to give our opinion as mental health workers.

Student F : Well, my first reaction was that she was a mentally ill woman.

Leader : We have to recognise that a person may be mentally ill in some senses and be beyond the reach of treatment because the person concerned does not look on it as illness and does not seek help.

Student H : We do not know for certain that it is her husband's child.

Student D : I cannot see why we should see her as a mentally ill person merely because she is rejecting her child. This is universal.

Leader : We spoke of the standards which we acquire. We have not yet discussed what the standards are and how they are acquired. It is necessary if you live in a community to have rules. We all of us have the capacity to take advantage of each other. The law alone isn't enough protection. There are many things which are not illegal which we just don't do to each other. For example, as children we don't split on each other and so on into adult life. Somehow or other, this woman has broken the rules. Is this an illness? There were times when only physical illness was regarded as sickness. Then mental symptoms became accepted as a medical responsibility. Only recently have we begun to adopt the concept of social illness in an individual who has not developed the ordinary social standards.

Student A : Mrs. Y has now changed her mind about her baby.

Leader : This may be just as pathological as her initial refusal to bring it up herself.

Student J : I wonder if she would have done this if she had been a Roman Catholic?

Student G : Could we assume that if she were a Roman Catholic and she had done this she would have been mentally ill?

Student B : I cannot see that that is anything to do with it.

Student J : Suppose that the mother had been a Catholic and the child had been given to a convent; what would have happened then?

Leader : I think that brings up another point. There are cultures that are characterised by certain attitudes to child rearing. We have a certain idea in mind as to what the English attitude to bringing up children is. There are some more uniform cultures which have been studied by anthropologists in some areas of New Guinea. Different tribes live quite near to each other with absolutely different ideas on child rearing. In one culture, the children are treated gently and are well and carefully looked after. They grow up into peace-loving adults. In another tribe, however, the children are treated aggressively. They are fed and then bustled away, the parents never spend a lot of time with them and they are treated abruptly. In both tribes, however, there are deviants. It has been said that if the aggressive person was moved out of the gentle tribe into the more aggressive one, he would be happier there. But I do not think so. I think the whole essence of the behaviour is in the fact that it is deviant.

The Chinese and the Japanese are a similar kind of example. In China, children were brought up with a good deal of tolerance and showed no anxiety such as we know in the Western world. As adults, they were serene, peace-loving people. In Japan, the children were brought up aggressively, almost cruelly, and they became a war-like nation. So what is normal depends upon the culture.

Student A : Is it not true that the Japanese introduced some heroic deeds deliberately into their myths and legends to make the children more aggressive?

Leader : Yes. That is directed aggression.

Student L : I wonder whether in the case of the baby farms which Hitler introduced into his régime the girls were right or the dictator?

Leader : I think that there are occasions when we must ask ourselves whether the deviant is "normal" or the people who fit in with the culture. There are people who differed from the social culture of their day who have been the forerunners of a new social system.

Student J : It is said that mentally ill people sometimes see things more clearly.

Student E : There is a story told about the psychiatrist who examined his patient, and at the end of the interview the patient said, "Well, I have listened to you and you have listened to me, and my conclusion is that it is you who is mad!"

Student A : There is another article in the press this morning about a difficulty between teachers : where some teachers are saying that men teachers only should teach in boys schools and women teachers in girls' schools. Would you like to comment on this?

Leader : I think we will let that come up when we are dealing with the child of school age. We must stop at this point.

This record of one session of a particular discussion group shows, firstly, the members of the group reacting spontaneously, even forcefully, towards a case that did not come from the professional area of their lives but from the private and personal area, i.e. from their daily newspaper reading. Members of a group, even a group of professional people, and not always excepting the leader, are likely to respond to such stimulus as members of the newspaper-reading public, escaping from the protection or restraint that they derive from their professional framework.

We have already mentioned one important aspect of Group Discussion leader's function as being the making of links and the pointing out of particular connections. To do this, he must select what seems to be most relevant to the group at the time from a complex and varied field. In the particular instance we are considering, the links that he made are those between the professional and the personal areas of social workers' experience. Here the leader had first of all to make it possible for the members of the group to reveal their own personal attitudes to the topic under discussion; when they had done this he was able to relate these attitudes to the professionalised and theoretical formulations, and to attempt to bring them all into the same framework. The technique he adopted in order to confront them with the same phenomenon in a personal as well as in a professional context was almost too successful, and there was subsequent difficulty in trying to return to the use of professional concepts. Individual personal bias was shown so freely, and the divergence of views at one point became so great, that it needed a joke, producing laughter in which all could share, to restore a measure of group cohesion. In the course of the heated discussion, a good deal of hostility was expressed, much of it directed openly or covertly at the leader. Some of this was resolved within the natural action of the group, and some of it was diverted by the introduction of some intellectual themes that were relevant to the topic. At the end of the session one member maintained his independence of the psychiatric challenge to previous attitudes by telling a story at the expense of the group leader. He was allowed to have what was effectively the last word.

The dichotomy between professional and personal attitudes may be more than usually clear-cut in our example, in which the behaviour that is being considered falls outside the range considered as normal. The professional worker in the mental health field is asked to explain such behaviour in terms which help him to deal with it, but he has been accustomed to observing the same behaviour as an ordinary member of the public, making judgements upon it and dealing with it in traditional ways. He may come to substitute a professional language for stereotyped popular explanations, and then proceed to use the professional language in exactly the same way, i.e. to supply a label which serves instead of an attempt to understand the behaviour at a deeper level. The *professional* labels, such as "frustration", "anxiety", "conflict", "oedipal conflict", and the rest, may be no more explanatory than the *popular* labels such as "incompetence", "laziness", and "wickedness".

The use of stereotyped labels of one sort or another has a purpose. If it does not provide an explanation, it may relieve one of the burden of finding an explanation. In a group, it is also likely to be part of an attempt to solve a particular problem or to meet a particular need at an individual and at a group level. It may help to provide a period of apparent cohesiveness, a safe channel for the expression of a feeling, in a group that is not yet ready for deeper exploration or exposure. It may represent an attempt to toe an imaginary "party line", to demonstrate an acceptance of a particular school of thought.

If such labels continue to be used, and no other member of the group is able to challenge or repudiate them, it will become the task of the leader to do so. He will have to look for the reason behind the continuing use of these labels, and relate it to the total position in the group, to the way in which the group processes are operating, and to the attitudes open and covert, towards himself as leader. He may, as we have illustrated, respond to the situation by introducing new material which cannot be treated in quite the same way. Or he may make a more direct approach, pointing to the relationship, or lack of relationship, that has been shown between the use of stereotyped labels on the one hand, and the private attitudes to professional tasks on the other. There are certain questions that he might ask. These include "What additional information does the use of this term give us?", "What further information do we need, and for what purpose?", and "Can we put this into other words?"

It is likely that the leader of a discussion group will be working within a narrow time schedule, taking part in a course of fixed and limited duration; he may have to bear the requirements of a particular syllabus in mind, and remember the precedent set by the degree of progress a previous group achieved. He will wish to promote the development of his group as quickly as possible. But although he may be required to intervene more frequently and more directly than either a group psychotherapist or a group counsellor would be likely to do, he is also bound by many of the same considerations. All group work requires that the major element through which psychotherapy, counselling, or teaching is provided should be the action of the group itself. In every case, the group must be given opportunities to solve its own problems, and establish its own methods of working. The group discussion leader who exerts too great an influence over the group defeats the group's own purpose, and unwittingly replaces Group Discussion with a form of that very didactic teaching that it is designed to avoid.

The particular problems which all groups, and particularly such relatively unstructured ones, will have to solve are likely to be influenced and even intensified in the case of Group Discussion by the nature of the task before the group and the type of theme or topic on which each session is focused. Both these factors may increase the stress which is experienced by the individual members, and this increase is likely to be reflected in a strengthening of disruptive, as opposed to cohesive, forces in the group as a whole.

The task before a discussion group, within our use of the term, is to learn about some aspect of human behaviour in which the behaviour of each individual member is inevitably included. Such learning requires involvement at emotional as well as at intellectual levels. The success of the learning process can best be evaluated by the nature and extent of the modification that takes place in each member's subsequent behaviour.

How far this expectation can be made explicit at the

beginning will depend upon the nature, purpose, composition, and level of sophistication, of each particular discussion group. It cannot be determined by intellectual level alone, although some professional groups, whose members have had previous training in this field, could be expected to be more at ease with the concepts involved than others would be. The idea that the provision of opportunities for personal change is an aim of Group Discussion is an idea that could be misinterpreted at different levels and in different ways. There is a danger that it may be taken to mean change in some predetermined direction imposed by the leader, and even the leaders of discussion groups have sometimes appeared to see their role in this light. There may be, as has already been stated, some members of a group who have come to teach what they know already rather than to learn, or who are primarily concerned with the defence of existing standards which give them worth in their own or in other people's eyes. The leader of a discussion group may have little or no opportunity to influence the selection of members, either in terms of personal suitability, or in order to try to secure a homogeneous group, a diverse group, or a group selected according to any other particular principle. To a greater extent than the group psychotherapist or the group counsellor, the discussion group leader may have to accept all comers, and to find some way of accommodating them within the group. Therefore in Group Discussion, the leader may encounter difficulties in making the purposes and process explicit, at least in the initial stages, and these may have to be discovered by degrees. The other two systems are less likely to be hampered in this way.

Whatever the way in which the idea of change is formulated and understood, the members of discussion groups are likely to feel themselves faced with a new and challenging situation. The stress entailed in such discussions is particularly evident in such courses as the one for mental welfare officers already described. These experienced workers had already established their own methods of work, from which they were able to get some satisfaction, without the benefit of formal training; they were now exposed to a situation in which these methods were being questioned. The problems that this created for them, and the attempts to find solutions for these problems, contributed to the establishment of a characteristic pattern of behaviour throughout each course which became very apparent after experience of a number of such courses in successive years.

Each course, apparently irrespective of whether its length was one day or several days, weeks, or even months, seemed to be marked by four successive stages. In the first stage, an apparently united and enthusiastic group showed its readiness to accept new knowledge in the hope and expectation that this would change the whole pattern of previous work and answer all the problems hitherto found insoluble. The second stage was marked by growing disappointment with what was being provided, and the development of a critical attitude to the ideas that were being communicated. In the third stage open hostility was shown to the leaders, tutors, and lecturers, coupled with an apparent belief that a "party line" was being put forward and that opposition to it would be interpreted unfavourably; sometimes there were two factions, the second opposing the first and expressing enthusiastic loyalty to the "party line". In the fourth stage there was a shift to a position in which much of the initial ambitions and expectations was relinquished, in which small changes of viewpoint could be accepted, and a few new ideas incorporated into a framework which also included previous personal and professional experience.

There were differences in the extent to which each individual student managed to work through the difficulties of each of these four stages, and to make a final adjustment. There were some who remained at any one of the previous three stages, who left the course still waiting to receive "the message", or who were under the impression that they had found it, or who were still vigorously opposed to new explanations which they could not reconcile with those they had accepted in the past. There were some, again, who mastered the jargon and remained satisfied with this, using it more enthusiastically than their teachers ever did. All these students would return to their jobs with a fresh entitlement to success, and a need to find fresh explanations for their failures. But if these students are considered to be the failures of the group, then what, may we ask, is the explanation or excuse of the group leader?

In spite of the importance of the position of the group leader, and the significance of his contributions, the problems that the group has to tackle cannot be solved by him alone. Like every other living organism, a group cannot by-pass necessary stages of development. Neither can the *pace* at which a group as a whole progresses be able to take sufficient account of the particular needs of each individual member. The leader may suggest solutions, but he cannot impose them. Whatever each group's particular aim may be, some will be less successful in achieving it than others, and even successful groups will contain individual failures. Failures may have to be tolerated by a Group Discussion leader, just as the psychotherapist has to tolerate clinical failures.

In Group Discussion each session is likely to be focused upon a particular topic, chosen perhaps by the leader, perhaps by the members, or determined by the demands of a particular syllabus. This topic will have its impact upon the behaviour of the group.

"Parental Rejection of the Infant" is a theme likely to arouse strong feelings and painful associations even among experienced workers. The experience of rejection is universal. All have some share in the condition both of the rejected child and of the rejecting parent or substitute parent figure. The mental welfare officers, temporarily *in statu pupillari*, were at that time playing the role of children *vis-à-vis* their lecturers and tutors, and were sensitive to rejection from this quarter.

They were engaged in considering themselves as social workers, members of a caring profession with clients who would sometimes experience them as rejecting. From both these points of view it was clearly a disturbing theme, and this is reflected in the behaviour of the group and in the relationship between the group members and the group leader. Both of these would have been different in response to a different topic.

Reading the record, one sees that some members of the group found it necessary to repudiate the behaviour of Mrs. Y in the strongest terms. Because of this, they were unable to consider her as a potential client, or to look for alternative explanations of her behaviour and of their reactions to it, and the attempts of the group leader to return the discussion to a professional framework were resisted.

Another feature which needs to be considered in this context is the hostility that this particular group expressed towards their leader. Though this behaviour has several aspects, as has already been indicated, it also needs to be related to the particular group theme. The final repudiation of the leader in his profession of psychiatrist, though voiced by only one member, was contradicted by none, and it seems legitimate, therefore, to regard it as an expression of some more general group feeling. It was only paralleled by the equal repudiation of Mrs. Y as a person who deserved consideration and understanding. The leader had presented them with a disturbing experience, and they behaved to him in the same way that they were behaving towards the rejecting parent. In response to the theme "Parental Rejection of the Infant", they behaved as if they themselves felt like unwanted children.

In the relationship between the group leader and the members of a discussion group there are present many of the same elements as in the relationship between parent and child or therapist and patient. The leader must be cautious of using this fact in interpretation. In many situations the students would resent comparison with either patients or children—it is

quite bad enough to be students! Furthermore, such interpretations might bring specific relationships within the group
into the area of discussion, focusing upon feelings towards the
leader with a particularity likely to be inappropriate in this
context. It is important, nevertheless, that the leader should
recognise that he is himself subject to the same conflicts with
his students as he would be with his patients or with his own
children, and as he was with his parents and with his tutors
and therapists. He must consider whatever role he may feel
required to adopt in the group with this in mind; and he must
understand that the disruptive and cohesive forces existing in
the group are likely to be exhibited through opposition and
alliance to the leader, to his person, to his topic, and also to his
profession where it differs from that of the rest of the group.
This is a situation which he shares to some extent with group
psychotherapists and group counsellors. The difference lies in
the use that he makes of it. The leader is aware that the
students are responding to the particular topic at issue within
a particular context, and that a major part of that context
consists of the relationship that they have with him, in
phantasy and in reality. But since this is Group Discussion,
his aim is not concerned with specific personal problems and
relationships. His aim is to enable the discussion to proceed
in such a way that it will provide a positive and relevant
learning opportunity for the members of the group, within the
limits of what has been sanctioned. For this reason and for
this purpose his interpretations, if he chooses to make interpretations, are not to an individual personality nor necessarily to
relationships in the group as a whole; rather, they are directed
to the topic that is being discussed and its implications for
them all.

Whatever use the group leader decides to make of his
relationship with the members of the group, and this will
depend upon its direct relevance to the group's topic, the
maturity and strengths of the group, and its readiness to look
at its own behaviour, he must bear in mind another function

with which he is invested. He is expected to provide a model with which members of the group may identify. Since Group Discussion is concerned with some aspect of human behaviour, including interpersonal relationships, the group leader will be looked upon as embodying and exemplifying that aspect of human relationships which is contained within the group theme. This is an aspect of the group leader's role which can provide him with an effective teaching tool. This is expressed by Balint in his account of groups designed to help general practitioners to become more sensitive to their patients' problems. He writes thus of the role of the leader in these groups. "By allowing everybody to be themselves, to have their say in their own way and in their own time, by watching for proper cues—that is speaking only when something is *really* expected from him and making his point in a form which, instead of prescribing *the* right way, opens up possibilities for the doctors to discover by themselves *some* right way of dealing with the patient's problems—the leader can demonstrate in the 'here and now' situation what he wants to teach."[1]

The model that the leader wishes to supply may differ from that which the group assumes he is supplying. Either model may be tested for flaws. A group of young people may attempt to shock or disconcert a group leader, or enquire into his private life, in order to test his sincerity. The leader of a group of social workers may find that he is expected to demonstrate an invariably accepting and non-judgemental attitude, and he may be presented with case histories of great length and complexity so that he may continue to listen with unwearied patience and attention. There are circumstances in which it is neither necessary nor desirable that the group's expectations should be met.

The particular topic that is under discussion at any moment in time will supply another reference for the model that the

[1] Michael Balint, *The Doctor, the Patient, and his Illness*, Pitman, 1957.

leader is expected or assumed to be supplying. With this aspect of the leader's role in mind, we can suggest another explanation for the hostility that the mental welfare officers showed to their leader. Their behaviour may be considered as representing a challenge to the personal position the leader had taken up towards the group topic. The members of the group are disturbed by the discussion of parental rejection, in the particular way in which it has been presented to them by the leader, and in the particular circumstances of this group. The anxiety that is aroused is painful, and they look for a way to relieve it. The way they find is to treat the rejecting person as someone who is beyond the pale, but this is a solution to their problem that the leader tries to deny them.

In effect, a dialogue takes place between the group members and the group leader which could be summarised as something like this:

Group members: The situation you have presented to us is too disturbing. We do not wish to consider it as a part of human experience. We wish to be able to treat the rejecting parent as an outcast and have nothing to do with her.

Leader: The behaviour that has been described is part of human experience and is part of your professional concern. It cannot be separated out and disregarded. Nor need it be. There are other ways in which we can handle it.

Group members: Then you must show us these other ways and make good your claim. We will reject you, and thus give you an opportunity to show us how rejection can be handled.

Several different explanations have now been suggested for the hostility shown to the leader in this group. These explanations are not alternatives, and no one explanation is likely to be sufficient. Any behaviour that actually takes place in a group is an end result of a combination of many different factors. This combination of factors is very complex. Yet, in looking for the cause of any single event, it is important that the leader should not overlook the more open and immediate ones. In our example, it may be thought that the story attacking the group leader as a psychiatrist was a not inappropriate response to his gratuitious introduction of some lengthy and perhaps boring anthropological explanations.

The assimilation of new ideas and the reorientation of attitudes is a process that cannot be imposed or hurried. Within the Group Discussion context, the members need to have opportunities to explore and experiment freely, to discuss and try out new concepts. Interventions from the group leader may serve to distort rather than foster the natural development of the group. Nevertheless, the purpose is education, and experiences in the group are of value to the extent that they can be used as part of an educational process. The leader is always there as a teacher and he has to see that learning can take place in the group. For this purpose, he is likely to intervene more frequently and more directively than a group psychotherapist or group counsellor would be likely to do. "Reliance on the untrammelled operation of group forces" and "confidence in the group's capacity to solve its own problems" could be explanations offered by inexperienced leaders to account for inadequate leadership. Group Discussion may, in fact, never become established in those groups where the leader elects to play a very passive role, perhaps modelled on that of certain group psychotherapists he has known, but transferred to a situation where conditions for the practice of Group Psychotherapy are absent.

In all the groups we are considering, one can envisage situations in which the groups may attempt to solve an immediate problem by adopting or permitting methods of behaviour inimicable to the very purpose of the group. The solution may be a temporary one, which will be abandoned spontaneously with the next step in the group's development. It may, in contrast, be prolonged to the point where the leader finds it necessary to intervene. In Group Discussion, the intervention of the leader is likely to occur at an earlier stage than in the other two systems. The danger the leader has to see and forestall is in the establishment of a permanent "culture" or habitual mode of behaviour, which will prevent the group from carrying out its particular function. This may happen if freedom of discussion becomes seriously limited, if certain conventions of speech and behaviour come to be imposed, and if certain topics, or the contributions of certain members, are not allowed. It may happen when a single member, or a sub-group, come to dominate the proceedings, and other members permit this or find that they cannot deal with it.

The techniques that a group leader might use in these situations can be discussed most readily in connection with Group Discussion. Indeed, we cauld not presume to be so specific about the role of the leader in either of the other two systems. But the leader of a discussion group has an obligation to teach, and to create and maintain a learning situation, and he may be having to operate within a tight time schedule. In addition, the relationships within the group are nearer to the realities of everyday life, and so permit his more direct intervention. Group counsellors and group psychotherapists should be able to learn something from considering the methods of Group Discussion, but their own techniques have to be selected according to other criteria and to serve other purposes.

There is, for example, the situation in which the group allows itself to be dominated by a monopolist. The monopolist, and there may be more than one if this is not a contradiction in terms, may introduce a theme himself, or may use one supplied by someone else, as a vehicle for the transmission of his views. He may attempt to keep the whole of the discussion period focused upon the theme he has introduced or selected, and effectively impede the introduction of other themes and other aspects. He may direct his remarks to another member or to the leader, and use the response he receives, whatever it may be, for a reaffirmation of his viewpoint in a slightly different form, or as an opening which permits him to produce new examples. The topic he selects may be an interesting and important one, and the leader may feel tempted to deal with it if it seems relevant to the group and provides an opportunity for debate. Other members may tolerate or even enjoy this for a time, but eventually they will feel that they are being by-passed and excluded from the discussion. This behaviour on the part of different individuals and of the group as a whole will have its explanations, and the leader needs to try and find these; however, he may also need to have to hand a practical technique for dealing with it. This could be simply to allow such a member to have a second question or interjection as a supplementary to the original one, and then, at his third contribution, to say, "Let us leave this for the time being; we will return to it" (and this promise must be kept), and then, "Can we have another example?", addressing the members of the group comprehensively. If this is done, it becomes the duty of the group leader at some stage to find some connecting links between the subsequent discussion and the first contribution.

Another situation that poses its own problems is the presence of a "paranoid" member within the group, and indeed nearly every discussion group contrives to include in its midst some-one who demonstrates these personal attitudes, although the term "paranoid" is not intended in any clinical sense. Such a person is likely to find fault with every formulation, represent-ing it as an example, in one way or another, of the damaging effect of external forces upon individual behaviour. He may relate causes of difficulties under discussion to "society", to inheritance, to class influences, to economic conditions, or, in a more general way, to established authority. His views may lead to divisions in the group, drawing hostility from some members and support from others. He may even succeed in eliciting from the group as a whole compassionate attempts to make up for the deprivation he has so obviously suffered. The leader may be tempted to try to satisfy or even "cure" him. Alternatively, the leader may find himself doing battle with this member, with supporters and opponents among the others,

and may seek to exclude him, or to bring about his withdrawal. We can hazard a guess, however, that if this member
were to withdraw because of action taken by the leader alone,
another would be likely to take his place. His behaviour must
have meaning for the other members who permit it, and who
oppose it, and may represent some aspect of their situation
that they wish to have expressed.

Apart from expressing this general aspect, such a member
should be looked upon as valuable to the proceedings. He can
penetrate the falsity of many established views which might
otherwise be accepted uncritically by other members and even
by the leader. He can challenge the leader's statements, and
is able to prevent an easy and shallow acceptance, by the
majority, of points which the leader puts forward. Such a
person must therefore be listened to, and the leader must be
prepared to be surprised at the validity of some of this
member's contributions, and the comparative inappropriate-
ness of some of his own.

If, as may happen, some of this "paranoid" member's
contributions seem a little odd, it can be a task of the leader
to add something to them and give them a structure that will
fit into the general theme. Some of these contributions may
be disturbing, and the leader will have to repair the situation
by remarks which also add something to it. Essentially, these
remarks begin with the word "Yes", and not with "Yes,
but . . ." but with "Yes, and . . .". Thus they are used to
demonstrate the possibility of a response to the unanticipated,
and a readiness to find creativity in something presented in
an unfamiliar way. This is one of the functions of the teacher
which goes beyond imparting given knowledge. It applies also
to the parent who takes the child's first babbling sounds and
makes them into words. In an incidental way this may be
"therapeutic", but it is still related to education more than
to any other primary process.

There is still the problem of the other members' position in
this situation. They may openly express frustration, but it is

likely that there will be some recognition of the fact that this awkward and argumentative member also speaks for them. The leader's tolerance (which need not be unbounded) is in the long run reassuring to the other members of the group. And perhaps they are glad that one member is prepared to stick his neck out and be the one to risk having his head cut off.

CHAPTER 8

In Conclusion

IN CONCLUSION, we return again to the group leader, and the central position that he occupies in all groups. Members may join a group with ideas about its purposes and processes that are distorted, inaccurate, and incomplete; the responsibility is not theirs. The responsibility belongs to the leader, and it is his ideas that must be clear. His perception of the group is all-important, and determines much of what will follow.

A central theme of this book has been composed of an attempt to distinguish between different forms of group work. For this purpose we have divided groups into three different categories. The dangers of a blurring of boundaries and consequent confusion as to what is, or should be, taking place in a group are very real. In each of the three systems of group work that we have described, the actual proceedings of the group, and the group processes taking place, form a principal vehicle through which the purpose of the group is achieved. In all three, the leader is required to recognise, understand, and in some way influence, these proceedings and processes without unnecessarily distorting or hindering their natural development. He does so in the context of the particular aims of the group and within the limits of what has been sanctioned. Some of the different ways in which this may be attempted have been discussed in reference to the three systems. But it is impossible to say that any one technique belongs exclusively to one particularly system and has no place in another. We cannot say, for example, that intepretation is a technique of

Group Psychotherapy, and that direct intervention to divert the course of the proceedings of the group from a particular path can only be considered in Group Discussion. This lack of technical demarcation highlights the importance of a clear conceptual basis in every instance, rooted in an understanding of aims and limits. Any group leader, for example, may use interpretation as part of his technique, but it is essential that he should know what particular end the interpretation is serving, whether of Group Discussion, Group Counselling, or Group Psychotherapy.

A group leader, no matter what group he leads, has responsibility for seeing that the group exists as a group, and not as a mere conglomeration of separate individuals or a collection of sub-groups. His foremost duty is to help the group to function. Every leader has to lead, and even in a psychotherapeutic group with unrestricted verbal interchanges, he still has to impose some limitations upon what takes place. He occupies a very particular and important role. Even though members and leader are arranged in a circle, the point on the circumference where the leader sits becomes a special position.

Remembering his special role, there are certain types of behaviour that every group leader must avoid lest he distort or inhibit the spontaneous group development that is needed. The leader must make communications to the group, but he attempts to make communications in such a way that they are not addressed with any particularity; rather, they are thrown into the middle of the group so that any member may be allowed to pick them up. When questioned, the leader must answer, but he should answer incompletely in order to allow further comments on the same topic. A complete answer from the leader silences the group.

In all the groups we are discussing, periods of silence are likely to occur. They should be permitted but not insisted on. The leader will not be in a hurry to break a silence, neither will he permit it to continue so long that it arouses anxiety that is inappropriate to the circumstances of his particular group. He will need to try to understand the meaning of the silence. There are hostile silences, thoughtful silences, and those silences which are a consummation. A hostile silence may need an interpretation to permit the group to proceed. A thoughtful one may need an interruption, since the members may feel, as the length of the silence increases, that the value of the next contribution must attain an increasingly high level. The silence which is a consummation may need to continue until the group feels itself ready for a fresh experience.

Communications from the group leader are likely to take the form of questions rather than statements. Questions open doors in situations where statements would only close them. Questions will be used to point out certain links and make certain connections. This has already been discussed in relation to Group Discussion, but it applies equally to all the three systems, although the links and connections will be different ones.

The Group Discussion leader will ask *"What else?"* Focusing upon the group topic, his questions will be "In what other context . . . related to what other themes . . . for what other purposes?" The group counsellor will ask *"How else?"* or *"Who else?"*. "How else do you think such a situation may be handled, and with what result . . . how might this seem to other people?" The question "Who else . . .?" can be used to bring other participants into the discussion and to illustrate the universality of a problem. The question "When else?" can be used to elicit the connections of any event with similar examples in the history of individual members. The characteristic question of the group psychotherapist, with the least direct focus but the greatest particularity, is *"How come?"*. This question leads directly to the unconscious processes.

The questions are likely to be phrased in such a way that any personal attribution is minimised. For example, the question is not "How do *you* feel?", but "How does this sort of thing affect *people*?"; it is not "How did you deal with it?", but "How have different people dealt with it?", "Does it make sense to do this or to do that?", "Is there another problem that is similar?", "Is there a different problem?". These may be the questions that would be most frequently asked by a group counsellor, but they illustrate the generality that belongs to all groups.

And if the reader disagrees, as well he may, we would ask "How would *he* interpret these questions?", and "What questions would he ask *instead* of them? Or *in addition*?". In fact, more simply, "*What else?*"

Bibliography

BALINT, M., *The Doctor, the Patient, and his Illness*, Pitman, 1957.

BERNE, ERIC, *Games People Play*, Grove Press Inc., 1967.

BERNE, ERIC, *The Structure and Dynamics of Organisations and Groups*, J. B. Lippingcott Company, Philadelphia, 1963.

BION, W. R., Group dynamics : a re-view, *International Journal of Psychoanalysis*, Vol. 33, 1952.

BION, W. R., *Experiences in Groups*, Tavistock Publications, 1961.

BOWLBY, J., *Child Care and the Growth of Love*, Penguin Books, 1965.

COYLE, G., *Group Work with American Youth*, Harper, 1948.

EZRIEL, H., A psychoanalytic approach to group treatment, *British Journal of Medical Psychology*, Vol. XXIII, Parts 1 and 2, 1950.

EZRIEL, H., The role of transference in psychoanalytic and other approaches to group treatment, *Acta Psychotherapeutica*, Supplement to Vol. 7, 1959.

FENICHEL, B., *The Psycho-analytic Theory of Neurosis*, W. Norton & Co., New York, 1945.

FERRARD, MARGARET L. and HUNNYBUN, NOEL K., *The Caseworker's Use of Relationships*, Tavistock Publications, 1962.

FOULKES, S. H., *Therapeutic Group Analysis*, Allen & Unwin, 1964.

FOULKES, S. H. and ANTHONY, E. J., *Group Psychotherapy. The Psycho-analytic Approach*, Penguin Books, 1957.

FREEMAN, H. and FARNDALE, J., *New Aspects of the Mental Health Services*, Pergamon Press, 1964.

FREUD, S., *Collected Papers*, Vols 1-4, Hogarth Press, 1948.

GLOVER, E., *Psycho-analysis*, 2nd edition, Staples Press, 1949.

GREENSON, R. H., *The Technique and Practice of Psychoanalysis*, Vol. 1, Hogarth Press, 1967.

HALMOS, PAUL, *The Faith of the Counsellors*, Constable, 1965.

JOHNS, T., T group traumas, *Journal of Institute of Personnel Management*, Vol. 1, No. 7, 1968.

JONES, MAXWELL, *Social Psychiatry*, Tavistock Publications, 1952.

KAHN, J. H., *Human Growth and the Development of Personality*, Pergamon Press, 1965.

KAHN, J. H. and NURSTEN, JEAN P. N., *Unwillingly to School*, Pergamon Press, 2nd edition, 1968.

KAHN, J. H., The Newham Community Mental Health Service, in *New Aspects of the Mental Health Services*, Ed. Freeman, H. and Farndale, J., Pergamon Press, 1967.

KLEIN, JOSEPHINE, *The Study of Groups*, Routledge & Kegan Paul, 1956.

KLEIN, M., *The Adult World and Other Essays*, Heinemann, 1963.

KOFFKA, K., *Principles of Gestalt Psychology*, Harcourt Brace, New York, 1935.

KÖHLER, W., *Gestalt Psychology*, G. Bell, 1930.

MAIER, H. W., *Group Work as Part of Residential Treatment*, National Association of Social Workers, New York, 1965.

MORENO, J., *Who Shall Survive?*, Beacon, N.Y., 1953.

PARSLOE, P., Some thoughts on social group work, *British Journal of Psychiatric Social Work*, Vol. X, No. 1, 1969.

RICE, A. K., *Learning for Leadership*, Tavistock Publications, 1965.

SEGAL, H., *Introduction to the Theories of Melanie Klein*, Heinemann, 1964.

SLAVSON, S. R. (one of his books?), *Analytic Group Psychotherapy with Children, Adolescents and Adults*, N.Y. Columbia University Press, 1950.

STOCK WHITAKER, D. and LIEBERMAN, M. A., *Psychotherapy through the Group Process*, Tavistock Publications, 1965, and Atherton Press, New York.

THOMPSON, S., Working with families in a community service, *British Journal of Psychiatric Social Work*, Vol. VIII, No. 4, 1966.

Index

References in italic type refer to main sections of the book

Index

Some other Pergamon Press titles of interest

R. FOREN and R. BAILEY
Authority in Social Casework

B. J. HERAUD
Sociology and Social Work

B. KENT
Social Work Supervision in Practice

A. MUNRO and W. McCULLOCH
Psychiatry for Social Workers

For a list of titles and series
published by Pergamon Press,
please write, indicating your
particular field of interest, to
**The Marketing Department,
Pergamon Press Ltd.,
Headington Hill Hall,
Oxford OX3 0BW.**

Contents
of this Book

08 016219 3

58408

361.4
T37

Date Due

MAY 22 '78	DEC 0 4 '07		
MAR 14			
DEC 1 0 1985			
MAR 4 '95			
DEC 1 2 1995			
JAN 09 1996			
MAY 3 1 1996			
JUN 28 1996			
JUL 2 6 1996			
DEC 07 1996	FEB 9 00		
DE10 03			

NYACK MISSIONARY COLLEGE
NYACK, NEW YORK

 PRINTED IN U.S.A.